D0931429

THE CULTURED CLUB

Fabulous Fermentation Recipes

Dearbhla Reynolds

THE COUNTRYMAN PRESS
A division of W. W. Norton & Company
Independent Publishers Since 1923

Copyright © 2016 by Dearbhla Reynolds

Text by Dearbhla Reynolds
Photography © Joanne Murphy www.joanne-murphy.com
Design/styling/editing of the Irish edition by www.grahamthew.com/ Jette Virdi/ Kristin Jensen
Cover photograph by Joanne Murphy

First published by Gill Books, Dublin, Ireland. Gill Books is an imprint of M.H. Gill & Co.

For information about permission to reproduce selections from this book, write to
Permissions, The Countryman Press, 500 Fifth Avenue, New York, NY 10110

For information about special discounts for bulk purchases, please contact
W. W. Norton Special Sales at specialsales@wwnorton.com or 800-233-4830

Manufactured by RR Donnelley, Shenzhen

The Countryman Press
www.countrymanpress.com

A division of W. W. Norton & Company, Inc.
500 Fifth Avenue, New York, NY 10110
www.wwnorton.com

978-1-68268-245-6

10 9 8 7 6 5 4 3 2 1

Thank you for picking up this book and opening the space in your mind to embrace lost traditions and a story about food. It is an active step in appreciating the energy of food and it is a skill for life. It is one small suggestion of conscious consumerism. It is one small step in gaining a sense of sovereignty. Enjoy discovering a new cultural perspective.

Acknowledgments

While I must admit that the early years of *The Cultured Club* was a lonely path, this is ultimately an acknowledgment of gratitude to those who have shown up along the way. Be it big or be it small, their interest and questions have propelled me on. The greatest learning in life is from those we meet along the way, either to accompany us for part of the journey or to provide direction.

First thanks must go to my brave husband, Ed, who quickly had to come to terms with a rapidly transformed kitchen, away from the comforts of all that was familiar—and all of it unlabeled too. And so too to my children, dear love them, denied so much of the modern sweet palate but who know a good fermented dilly bean or sauerkraut and have a high tolerance for sour food. They have the greatest treat of all, which is a belly full of good friendly bacteria.

Thanks also to each and every person who has come to *The Cultured Club* to listen to the ancient wisdom of these foods. It has been a stimulating few years of sharing. Particular thanks has to be showered upon Laura and Alain Kerloch, firstly for their endless caring encouragement of a friend, so keen as I was to tell everyone about how great these foods are, and secondly for the invitation to host *The Cultured Club* courses at Michelin-star restaurant OX in Belfast. Both Alain and Stephen Toman at OX have continued to give their support to the growing revival of fermentation.

One of the advantages of following your heart and sharing your passion in life is that you meet like minds. In the endlessly connected story of food, I have met inspired folk such as Rita Wild and her fabulous Organic Box scheme, BOXA, who encouraged me to put food in a jar to sell.

Much of this food comes from John McCormack and his team at Helen's Bay Organic Gardens, who regularly give me the joy of jarring the glut of produce or saving misshapen goods from the compost heap. Further thanks goes to Simon Matthews and David Melville, who bring it to my loyal and enthusiastic customers at the market every week.

There would also be no sauerkraut if it were not for Roy Lytte and his fields of organic cabbages. Milk kefir would not exist without the cream raw milk from David Laughlin of Culmore Farm, Kilrea.

With enormous thanks, I am so grateful to Domini Kemp at Alchemy, Dublin, for hosting many a wonderful evening of fermentation fun.

Thanks also to Lady Fionnuala Aston Ardee at Kilruddery, for the annual workshops in such a glorious setting, and to Maggie Lynch and Richard Burton at IINH and all those who have so keenly hosted me around the country.

As we all know, word of mouth is the best recommendation. So without the kind referrals from holistic practitioners, health coaches, and nutritionists who have sent people my way, the word would never have spread about these naturally healing foods. Thank you Jane McClenaghan, Maria Rafferty, Dr. Finbar Magee, Jordan O'Donnell, David Hefferon, and Barbara Fabish in particular.

The creation of this book was a particular wish to fully express years of learning, experimenting, and tasting, and to impart an enthusiasm for feeling wonderful through food. This would not be possible without the wonderful team at Gill Books: Sarah Liddy, Teresa Daly, Ruth Mahony, Kristin Jensen, Jo Murphy, Jette Virdi, and Graham Thew, who made every step of the way a pure joy and fun. Thank you to editor Róisín Cameron, and the whole team at The Countryman Press in New York, for bringing this American edition into being. Thank you to Susan Jane White for the initial encouragement and Catherine Cleary for highlighting how significant this year has shaped up to be.

All those friends and family who have dined with me and been part of a taste test, without even knowing it. Thanks especially to Paul and Kinga, who always returned the dinner invite!

Thanks to Mark Van Laarhoven, for the greatest privilege to cater for his hungry earthship-building crew in Australia and receive such great feedback and encouragement.

To fully express all the gratitude would be another chapter, so for all those I have not personally mentioned, you all matter.

In advance of all the undiscovered places and projects I have yet to embark upon as I remain dedicated and true to the bacteria, which I rely on more so than they rely on me, I am truly excited that the world is rediscovering this lost skill again.

CONTENTS

INTRODUCTION

MY STORY

It's hard to really know where the inspiration for something so intrinsic stirs from until you are deep in the journey. It's only in retrospect that the obvious seems clear and the journey's meaning has conviction. Beyond being intrigued, I had no idea why I was choosing to forcibly rot all my food!

It all began when my life transitioned into motherhood. In motherhood, there is a meeting of one's own childhood, and as I now see it, this stands as an homage to my early childhood and my parents. Not many of us in Ireland grew up with these fiercely fermented, powerfully pungent foods. Perhaps the closest we came was the buttermilk mixed into the mashed potatoes or the smell of soda bread baking on the griddle.

To describe my childhood, it would taste of honey and home cooking. It would smell of a hearty stew and hedgerows coupled with the heady mix of iodine, ether, borax, liniments, and gauze from an old-school pharmacy.

One of my favorite things to do as a child was to accompany my father around the countryside with our heads in hedgerows, inspecting forageable goods and checking on his beehives. By day he was that old-school chemist, making and mixing tinctures and creams to heal the long line of customers waiting for their turn to tell him their woes; but by night, he was a honey maker and alchemist. Honey would be strained and some was always reserved for his hobby of making mead as he tinkered away with various airlocks and demijohns. For a pioneer, this was a dedicated hobby.

As I grew into my teenage years, I followed him into the pharmacy for an apprenticeship of sorts, with his hope that someday I would continue his legacy. However, there is clearly something more irresistible about honey and herbs than boxes of pills.

These memories are cozily nourished in the comforting smells and tastes of homemade cooking from my mother's kitchen. As a home economics teacher, she ran the home with dedicated attention. We knew our grocer, butcher, and milkman, and every meal was cooked from scratch. If we ate out once I must have missed it, as I have no recollection of it. I'm lucky that cooking skills were passed down daily, even if most were by observation or some kind of osmosis. Wherever I've gone, I have always felt equipped to decipher tastes and lodge them in my memory bank. Taste has a memory that we draw on continually as we eat and I bring all those edible flavors along.

These two early influences now seem inseparable.

When I discovered fermentation, it was no surprise to me that it should fit together in a complete understanding. There was an innocent fascination that kept me curious, but as I began to feel the benefits and became so consciously happy, I really got it—food is medicine. My childhood primed me for it. Using simple food science to make my medicine was the perfect marriage.

The dictionary definition of medicine states that it is "the science or practice of the diagnosis, treatment, and prevention of disease." As I mature, prevention is my motivation. The details of this book hover somewhere between home cooking, a curiosity for cheffy imagination, food science technique, and an unquestionable belief that food is a medicine that can promote great healing or cause great harm. It is radical home economics, which appeals to my renegade soul and the real pharmacist I was meant to be.

Perhaps, too, there is a hope that my children will be able to claim this as their heritage. How lucky for them that the scent of their childhood will be the pungent waft of kimchi or the tang of kombucha or that they happily drink beet kvass without even thinking twice. And they will be fiercely proud to eat, enjoy, and know this memory on their taste buds. I hope they agree. Goodness knows future generations need every bit of help they can get to navigate a path away from diabetes, for how we have cared for this community of bacteria living within and on us is not only important for our own health, but also for the generations to come.

WHAT IS FERMENTATION?

Fermentation is one of the oldest forms of food technology in the world. Native fermented foods have been prepared and consumed for thousands of years and are strongly linked to culture and tradition. Fermentation has been used for a long time as a perfect and low-cost way to preserve the quality and safety of foods throughout every native diet around the world. Essentially, the process of fermentation creates a controlled environment of decay during which the good bacteria flourish and act as a natural preservative. Tasty, right?

Am I talking about alcohol? Well, no, but also yes. There are research theories that say beer, not bread, is the reason early humans settled down and started farming around 10,000 years ago. It was an evolutionary turning point and a plausible concept.

The process of fermentation is a chemical alteration that transforms relatively complex compounds into simpler, more easily digestible compounds that provide digestive enzymes, friendly bacteria, vitamins, and other readily available nutrients.

Fermenting foods is mostly an anaerobic process, meaning without oxygen, carried out by micro-organisms or cells. These micro-organisms convert sugars and starches into other compounds, such as lactic acid, carbon dioxide, and alcohol.

Fermented foods are teeming with good bacteria and are rich in digestive enzymes. The abundance of digestive enzymes contributes to the processing of food in the body and the proper absorption of nutrients derived from food. Remarkable benefits can be experienced when you start to pay attention to this. Including a diverse daily serving of fermented foods can enhance immune system response, decrease irritation of the bowels, give you a healthy glow, provide digestive ease, give respiratory ease, decrease incidence of allergies and sensitivities, reduce sugar cravings, lessen incidence of bacterial infection, and contribute to a continual feeling of satisfaction, increased energy, better mood, mental clarity, and a general all-round feeling of well-being. While nothing is a magic bullet, it seems like a pretty good profile of benefits to me.

There is something to note, though. It's common to react to new probiotic foods with a gut-wrenching sensitivity. When you eat a new fermented food, you're basically bringing a whole new set of bacteria into a crowded situation in your gut. Depending on your current ecosystem, it could mean war for some! There is a detox reaction called the Herxheimer Reaction. It can be as bad as it sounds as the immune system reacts to the toxins that are released as the bad bacteria bid farewell. If the war must be waged with this sense of carnage, then taking it slowly—very slowly—is advised, but remain dedicated to a daily dose. By continually giving good bacteria the chance to dominate, over time your gut will settle down as the trillions of bacteria find a new equilibrium.

But a gut-wrenching reaction to a new ferment is actually a good thing! It means that you are slowly bringing your gut back into good health as the good probiotics take over. Never overdo it, though, as healing is a gradual thing. You may have many years of damage to correct, so it ain't gonna happen over the course of a week. Instead, start out by eating a small amount per day for a week and allow your hugely intelligent body to heal.

We have become scared of bacteria and obsessed with the pathogenic kind, which of course will make us sick. However, this doesn't take into account the billions of bacteria that are good for us and that we actually need to survive. We shouldn't be intimidated by the fermentation process or the word *bacteria*. Fermentation is actually quite simple and straightforward. It relies on little more than vegetables (or fruit) and salt. Worlds were discovered due to these white crystals, kingdoms were torn apart and powerful trade dynasties were established. Salt is essential to life. We cannot make it, yet our bodies need it.

There are tried-and-tested formulas for salt-to-water ratios that allow for the successful preservation of vegetables (see page 20). These must be observed in respect to the microbial chemistry that transforms these raw ingredients into supercharged superfoods teeming with good lactic acid bacteria. There are also flavors that work and those that don't, but fermentation is an art for you to discover, play with, and get your taste buds around.

THE THREE STAGES OF FERMENTATION

The process of fermentation is one of a microbial transformation, and in order for your fermented food to be a success, it goes through three stages.

During the first stage, the environment in the jar changes from aerobic to anaerobic thanks to bacteria that feed off any trapped oxygen. This allows the lactic acid bacteria to become established. This process takes between one and three days, depending on the temperature.

The lactic acid bacteria continue to develop during the second phase of fermentation. This stage can last anywhere between five and 30 days. Carbon dioxide is evident during this stage and the ferment looks very active. Low temperature or too much salt are the two things that will inhibit the growth of good bacteria. You can enjoy your ferment at this stage or leave it to develop even more bacteria.

Lastly, your fermented food will reach the maximum development of bacteria at around six weeks. It will have stopped producing carbon dioxide, hence bubbles, and it's ready for transferring to cold storage to halt fermentation.

These are some of the safest foods on the planet. Lactic acid fermentation is a well-documented process observed by scientists who have studied sauerkraut, kimchi, and other traditionally fermented vegetables.

OUR BACTERIAL ECOSYSTEM

Many who study the microbiome, our bacterial ecosystem, believe we are so deficient in a diversity of gut bacteria that we are experiencing a worrying extinction. We have a less diverse microbiome than our ancestors did, and yet we are also discovering that many different aspects of our health depend on this diversity. As our understanding shifts toward a greater appreciation of the human being as a composite organism, it would appear there is a lot happening within our guts, which are home to the trillions of micro-organisms called the microbiota and the two million genes they carry, called the microbiome. Scientific studies are revealing that the microbial ecosystem living in us and on us needs careful consideration, and how we address it is hugely influenced by diet, one forkful at a time. We are literally on the frontier of a new medical understanding.

For me, food is medicine. I make no bones about it—the food we eat maketh the man. Diet is the most important driver of microbiome composition in humans. If we put the wrong fuel in our car and all of a sudden it doesn't work, do we question the logic?

Regardless of the microbes you may not have inherited, what you feed the microbes living in and on you can make a big difference to how they behave. Even without fully understanding how the microbiome works, you can still push it in a healthier direction. While delving into the flavors and combinations of fermented goodness, this book will explore the benefits of these foods as an aid in cultivating a healthier community of microbes in your body.

THE CULTURE OF CULTURE

As a culture, we are defined by what we eat. Eating is a daily routine, a necessary ritual to fuel our bodies and give us the energy we need. However, for me there is a disconnect. We do not eat with this consideration. We do not eat for energy—most of the food we eat is to satisfy a craving as we ride a blood sugar roller coaster. Mostly we eat unconsciously and it is fueled by convenience, appeal, and the subtle psychological promises of advertising. Michael Pollan suggests that a lack of fermented foods is one of the most notable differences between the Western diet and all other successful diets throughout history.

Eastern European staples such as borscht and sauerkraut; the Korean staple kimchi; lassis and dosas from India; miso, tempehs, and tsukemono from Japan will never lose their place on the plate. It is the food that so uniquely defines their culture. For the rest of

us, we have lost touch with our land, our roots, and our soil. We have moved away from the small organic farmer to the supermarkets for our meals, putting the job of feeding millions of people into the hands of a few big businesses.

Today there is a fundamental need to rediscover food that makes us feel alive. Fermentation is moving beyond the realms of beer and wine and into the world of vegetables with the further revelation that these foods are enormously good for you. We are rediscovering traditions that historically were a necessary part of daily life. We forgot them as society moved out of the kitchen and into the workplace and life became more about convenience.

Fermentation is not a radical new diet, and hopefully it's not just a trend. It's a kitchen skill, just like using the oven or boiling an egg, that allows you to discover this lost food group and to make a place for it on the plate with all the other valued food groups. Whole food snacks and meals that can be created with ease, with consideration, and with soul.

My hope is that fermented foods become more than a fashionable fad, but rather a permanent feature on our plates once again. This book is an invitation to get involved with what we want and how we eat it. Let's celebrate the farmer, the grower, the beekeeper, and all those who play a part in cultivating our food.

Much of this book contains raw recipes, but there are many cooked meals too. The recipes are predominantly vegetarian with vegan alternatives. The dishes are dedicated to the millions of invisible bacteria that keep us well, and my aim is to illustrate how this technique complements and fits into all diets.

THE SCIENCE AND LORE OF THE KITCHEN

If fermentation is your first conscious exploration of food science, you will understand the fascination of this vast topic and how we are continually manipulating molecules. Food science is constantly evolving, with modern cuisine borrowing tools from the science lab and blending the laws of physics with chemical reactions. This creative explosion of food science and experimentation has created a very long list of restaurants one can only hope to dine at someday. Had I known that this type of chemistry was available to study, perhaps I would not have run so far away – maybe just as far as Copenhagen, to the Nordic Food Lab under the creative talents of René Redzepi and Lars Williams.

LOVE FOOD, HATE WASTE

A respect for food drives me to waste as little as possible. I don't even throw out avocado stones! These can be used sparingly, grated into smoothies and over salads. We can barely comprehend the global devastation that is food waste, but we all contribute to it. The point we are missing is that most of the time we are throwing away valuable nutrients and healthy goods. The recipes in this book include a focus on using up old brine or the discarded bits of veggies and fruits, even your eggshells, all of which can become part of your kitchen routine and your dinner. Fermented foods are the perfect way to waste less.

A NOTE ON INGREDIENTS

When fermenting, there are a few key ingredients, so choose wisely for successful fermentation and for your health. This exposes a few truths about our food industry and shatters a few illusions about healthy foods.

RAW HONEY

Not all honey is created equal. In fact, commercial honey has little or no traces of pollen in it, making it just golden sugar syrup. This "fake" honey won't produce the desired effects when making jun or honey ferments. Raw honey will be clearly stated as such or it will be from a local, small-scale producer. To test if your honey is fake or not, pour one tablespoon into a glass of water. Pure honey will clump together at the bottom of the glass, while fake honey will dissolve in the water.

RAW MILK

Pasteurised milk can be loaded with synthetic hormones and antibiotics. Further to this, the milk is homogenized, which destroys raw milk's natural butterfat in order to separate the cream. No, thank you. In the few recipes that include milk, it's better to use raw milk to enjoy a superior-tasting fermented result along with its increased benefits, such as more omega-3 fats, enzymes, vitamins, and healthy bacteria.

RAW APPLE CIDER VINEGAR

Raw apple cider vinegar is a living vinegar that still contains the bacteria, referred to as "the mother." This will be stated on the label. If it isn't, the apple cider vinegar you are buying is inert and does not contain any active ingredients. When a ferment recipe calls for apple cider vinegar, it's always preferable to use raw apple cider vinegar.

RAW CANE SUGAR

Raw cane sugar is dehydrated from cane juice and it is not refined, so it still contains the natural micronutrients but also the impurities. Cane sugar that is not raw can be slightly refined. It's desirable to get the most nutrient-dense form of sugar to feed your kefir grains and scoby, but it's not imperative.

ORGANIC FRUIT AND VEGETABLES

It is a personal preference to choose organic vegetables and fruit to ferment. Not only does this guarantee good quality and great taste, but it supports a system that is sustainable. I know that it's not always possible to get organic produce, but you can be consoled by the fact that studies are showing that there is a reduction in pesticide residues during fermentation and the lactic acid bacteria help detox the pesticides that do enter your body.

If buying organic stretches your budget too much, then at least trying to ensure that the most heavily sprayed foods on your shopping list are organic will make a huge difference. These are called "the dirty dozen" and the list includes apples, blueberries, celery, cucumbers, grapes, nectarines, peaches, peppers, potatoes, tomatoes, spinach, and strawberries.

Organic unwaxed lemons are especially important for recipes that use them whole, like the preserved lemons on page 97. They are grown without the use of synthetic herbicides and pesticides and they are not coated in a waxy layer, which would inhibit fermentation.

TEA

Tea is worth considering when purchasing it for use in a ferment, namely kombucha. Ideally, I prefer to use loose tea, but for accessibility and speed, teabags sometimes take preference. Proper storage of teabags in an airtight container is important so that the bags themselves don't develop mold.

SALT

All the recipes in this book require salt for the fermentation process. When used in the right proportions, salt creates an environment within which we are able to better control the growth of micro-organisms and have a successful ferment. I recommend using sea salt. Maldon sea salt works well, but ideally try to use sea salts found on islands off the Atlantic coast of France, known as Celtic sea salt, or Himalayan rock salt, which contain significant nutrients, including trace amounts of magnesium, potassium, and calcium. If you're feeling rather adventurous, you could even have a go at evaporating your own salt from seawater. See the salt ratios on page 20.

WATER

Up to 60 percent of the adult body is water, so any adjustment in healthy eating practices should really start here. All water used in fermentation should be filtered to remove the chlorine (and fluoride if this is in your tap water), as this will interfere with the process. Simple charcoal filters will remove the chlorine but not the fluoride, so a more enhanced filtration system is required with specific filters—I recommend a Berkey water filter.

GETTING STARTED

The many jars and bottles brewing may appear to be a million miles away from what your kitchen currently looks like, or perhaps you are ready to open those jars or soak those groats to create something special. Wherever you join me, it's a journey.

When I first started dabbling, it used to drive my husband crazy that nothing had a label. To be fair, he was right. How was he to know what was in the jars? It would have made life easier to have had a contents and date label on there (so, as a side note, buy some kitchen tape and a permanent marker to label your projects). But for me this was my dream come true: a fridge full of the finest foods and not a single label promoting a multinational company in sight. It was a small, rustic achievement for my autonomous mind!

I admit that fermentation takes a little effort. First it can take time to undo our fear of bacteria. It can take a huge mental shift and some subconscious reprogramming to really grasp the simplicity of the bacterial transformation that is happening and accept that it's completely safe.

There may also be a little bit of balancing out as the new bacteria make themselves at home. This sense of discomfort can easily inspire abandonment, but when you stick with it you will reap the rewards, and they are undeniably magic: feeling light, happy, connected, and engaged.

Returning to traditional foods and fermentation practices inspires a new approach to the food you choose to eat and generally results in a lot of your food preparation becoming an overnight thing, with bowls of this or that soaking or fermenting away while you sleep. It conflicts with the modern, pre-packed, pre-chopped, convenient approach we have understandably grown to adopt. I know convenience sells. But to compensate, whipping up a meal can be super quick, as the real food prep of soaking or fermenting has been happening over time.

Give yourself the chance to find your own routine in all of this. It takes less time than standing in the supermarket trying to decipher labels. I know where I would rather be. It can be a journey of taste as much as it can be a journey of food preservation, self-preservation, and healing. My hope is to make it easy. You can have something in a jar in the right liquid that will make delicious, healthy, probiotic food for you in less than five minutes.

FERMENTATION TECHNIQUES: YOUR NEW ALCHEMICAL TALENTS

Fermentation is a 7,000-year-old method that relies on little other than vegetables (or fruit) and salt. If you're feeling extravagant, spices can be thrown into the mix too, which we will explore in the recipes. But the most basic process is easy:

- Wash your veggies well. If you're using organic produce, it's fine to just wash them and not peel the fruit or vegetables unless they have really tough skins. If you're not using organic produce, then I recommend peeling it.
- Cut them up about the same size.
- Add seasoning (think garlic, ginger, apples, and spices like coriander, bay leaf, chili peppers, star anise, etc.).
- Add salt (generally 2 percent of the weight of the food being fermented).
- Mix, massage, or pound the vegetables with your hands until the vegetables have released their juices, then pack them into a crock or glass jar.
- Submerge the contents to keep the oxygen out using a weight.
- And then leave it to ferment for anything from three days to six weeks.

Simple, isn't it?

There are various options for fermenting, but we will first focus on the two main methods. The first one, as used in the krauts and kimchi, is called dry salting, whereby a brine is created using the liquid extracted from the vegetable, creating enough brine to submerge the vegetable. The desired salt-tolerant *Lactobacillus* strains will live and propagate in this brine.

The other brining method is more applicable to foods that are whole, hard, or chopped into chunks. In this case you must create a brine

solution for them to be submerged in. Vegetables can be fermented in brines from 1.5 percent to 5 percent salinity. A brine of 2 percent to 3 percent will tend to achieve the best ferment. Brines higher than 5 percent will interfere with bacterial activity and halt fermentation.

Until you're familiar with the measurement of your chosen type of salt, I recommend that you weigh it out in grams before using it, as different salts have different densities.

Salt ratios per 1 quart (about 4 cups) of filtered water:
- 2 percent = 19 grams or 1 tablespoon salt
- 2.5 percent = 24 grams or 1 tablespoon + 1 teaspoon salt
- 3.5 percent = 33 grams or 2 tablespoons salt
- 5 percent = 48 grams or 3 tablespoons salt

Just a few examples of successful 2 percent salinity ferments are carrots (sticks, shreds, or slices), broccoli, cauliflower, pearl onions, green beans, asparagus, deseeded green or red bell peppers, parsnips, kohlrabi, Jerusalem artichokes, whole zucchinis, sliced radishes, and whole small radishes and whole green tomatoes.

TEMPERATURE

In order for any fermentation to be successful, you need food, water, salt, warmth, and time. We've already talked about food, water, and salt. The bacteria involved in fermentation function best at a temperature range of 60°F to 75°F—in other words, room temperature. However, take seasonal variations in temperature into consideration. In the summer you might only need to ferment your sauerkraut for a few days rather than weeks, whereas in the winter culturing might be a little slow.

Fermented foods are stored in the fridge once they are ready to your liking. This slows the fermentation process, although they do still continue to ferment, albeit extremely slowly.

GLASS JARS OR FERMENTATION CROCKS

There are many different types of jars and fermenting vessels available to buy. The best-quality jars are the Italian jars, as they are made with a sturdy, lead-free glass. However, flip-top glass jars that seal very tightly (such as the Fido, Weck, or Le Parfait brands) must be "burped" every other day to allow the build-up of carbon dioxide from fermentation to escape. I have had continued success for small batch-making using the sealable jars from Ikea, which allow for some of that gas to escape. For larger batches of sauerkraut and kimchi, I prefer to use my countertop fermentation crock. A fermentation crock is a ceramic pot that comes with two half-circle weights. It allows you to ferment a large batch of kraut and kimchi, which improves the quality and consistency of a ferment as seemingly a bigger mass of food creates a more vigorous ferment and a greater population of good bacteria. When the fermentation process is complete, the ferment can be decanted from the crock into smaller screw-top jars that can be stored in the fridge. As fermenting increases in popularity, you can find them online at sites such as Amazon.

WEIGHTS

Whatever vessel you choose, one of the requirements for successful fermentation is to provide an anaerobic environment to prevent oxidation and mold. During fermentation, the food must be weighted to keep it submerged under the brine at all times, as the liquid brine is where fermentation occurs. Food that rises above the surface will not fully ferment and will also be at risk of oxidation and mold. There are many inventive ideas for weights:

- **Cabbage leaf:** Placing a cabbage leaf on top of your ferment and tucking the sides down works well. Occasionally a small weight will also be needed to keep the leaf in place.
- **Rocks:** The right size and shape rock will make a perfect weight. Be sure to boil them first for about 20 minutes to kill any competing or harmful bacteria.
- **Marbles tied in a cheesecloth or muslin:** Marbles work well because they can easily fit whatever size or shape jar you are using. Make sure that the marbles are paint- or glaze-free and lead-free.
- **Baking weights:** These can be used like marbles and placed inside a cloth or even a fine-mesh bag. If you don't already have any of these, they can be easily purchased online.

- **Plastic bag with brine:** Not my favorite option, but if you go for it, use brine in it, not water, in case the bag leaks.
- **Small jar or glass:** Ideally the jar should be just slightly smaller in diameter than the lid of your fermentation jar. It can be filled with water to give it more weight.
- **Plate:** When I ferment in a large crock, I place a plate on top of the vegetables, then a jar filled with water on top of that to hold it down.

The goal of fermentation is to create an environment that favors a good culture. If your ferment looks funny, smells funny, or tastes off, then don't eat it.

CLEANLINESS

I'm the first to admit that I am far from OCD sterile, but keeping everything you use for fermentation as clean as possible to avoid contamination is crucial. Washing your jars, utensils, and crocks with hot water is important, as is not using too much dish soap. If you have a dishwasher, that's a great way to ensure cleanliness. Clean your kitchen surfaces when starting a project too. The cleaner your environment, the better.

KITCHEN EQUIPMENT

What I love about fermenting is that it's a very inexpensive kitchen hobby to adopt. You need very little, really, to make delicious food, but as with all areas of interest, there are tools to make life easy. The following have become kitchen must-haves for me:

- A **water filter** is nearly a must-have. They can range from a simple Brita charcoal filter to something more advanced. Logic prevails as to which will give the best results. Chlorine is the main thing that you want to filter out of the equation, as it will affect the quality of a ferment. If you live in an area where fluoride is added to your water, then you will want to remove this too, regardless of whether or not you are fermenting.
- **Kitchen scales** are useful tools and an inexpensive investment. I tend to use them once at the start of a new batch of vegetables, but once I have measured the quantity, it often reverts to guesstimating

and cup measurements. Cup measurements are really my go-to. Precise digital scales for measuring small amounts are important for more advanced kitchen experiments.

- A **good blender** will take you to great culinary places. There are wonderful options available to suit any budget, from the NutriBullet all the way up to the Vitamix. A lot can be concealed using a blender, allowing you to create the best fast food on the planet, rich in enzymes, enriched vitamins, and amino acids, and most importantly, food teeming with good bacteria. Plus you can sneak it into the fussy eaters in the house without them really knowing.

- A **food processor** is useful for preparing your vegetables, especially if you're going to approach this with gusto and ferment everything. However, it's not completely necessary. For a long time, chopping vegetables by hand became my meditation.

- On that note, no kitchen should be without a **good chef's knife and sharpening stone**.

- Though not essential, a **dehydrator** is mentioned a few times in this book. I have never looked back since acquiring one and it is in regular use in my kitchen. In recipes that use one I've also included instructions for using an oven instead, but the results are never quite as crisp.

- Some **cheesecloth** or tightly woven unbleached cotton is very useful for straining liquids to make cheese.

- **Nut milk bags** are fine-mesh bags that catch all the nut pulp and give you a smooth milk. They are inexpensive and handy to line a jug with when making nut milk.

- Finally, if you have **a few large mixing bowls, a sieve, and some cloth napkins or coffee filters and rubber bands for covering**, you are pretty much good to go.

FERMENTATION FAQS

HOW DO YOU STERILIZE JARS?

It is sufficient to clean your jars for fermenting with hot water. If you are using soap, then make sure to thoroughly rinse the jars. If you have a dishwasher, then consider yourself lucky, as that will easily do the job!

CAN I USE PLASTIC CONTAINERS FOR MY FERMENTS?

Glass and ceramic are the vessels of choice for fermenting. Although there are many food grade containers available, I still have reservations about harmful chemicals potentially leeching out during the fermentation period.

WHY DO YOU NEED TO LEAVE SOME HEADSPACE AT THE TOP OF THE JARS?

Many vegetables expand during the fermentation process. Leaving a little room at the top of the jar (usually 1 inch) allows for this without causing any pressure to build up.

WHY DO THE JARS FIZZ AND BUBBLE OVER WHEN YOU OPEN THEM?

In certain styles of jars, such as the Korken jars from Ikea, the seal isn't that tight. As carbon dioxide gas is produced as a by-product, it tries to escape though any gap, and as it escapes it brings some liquid brine with it.

WHY DO YOU NEED TO "BURP" A JAR AND HOW DO YOU DO IT?

If you're using a tight seal flip-top jar, such as a Fido or Le Parfait jar, then giving your ferment a quick little "burp" a few days into the fermentation process will help release some of the built-up carbon dioxide. "Burping" a jar simply means opening the flip-top seal just enough to let any air escape, then tightly sealing it again. Do this every other day while the jar is actively fermenting.

WHERE IS THE BEST PLACE TO PUT MY JARS WHEN THEY'RE FERMENTING?

Ideally you should keep your fermentation experiments on the countertop out of direct sunlight (unless the recipe states otherwise), and usually at a stable temperature range of 60°F to 75°F (room temperature). It's also advisable to place them on a plate or in a bowl to catch any spillage that may occur during the early stage of fermenting.

WHY DO YOU STORE THE JARS IN THE FRIDGE ONCE YOU'RE HAPPY WITH THE FLAVOR?

Traditionally fermented foods were made in the autumn as a source of food for the winter. Once they were fermented, they would be kept in a root cellar in cold winter temperatures, which would slow fermentation and keep them for longer. Today we use fridges to do that job. The bacteria involved in fermentation prefer a minimum temperature of 60°F to a maximum temperature of 90°F to perform their task. Most ferments will keep for six months in the fridge, but even 12 months later, they are still safe to eat, just maybe not tasting quite as fantastic. Even so, we can still find a use for them.

WHY IS THERE IS MOLD ON MY SAUERKRAUT/KIMCHI?

It can happen that mold forms on a fermented food experiment. If you have used the correct salt ratio and submerged your foods in sufficient brine, then the only thing that could cause mold to form is oxygen. Mold is a sign that something has gone wrong, so you should not consume it. However, in the case of brined whole foods, such as dilly beans, beet kvass, etc., a white layer of "mold" can sometimes be seen to appear. This is friendly kahm yeast and it can simply be scooped or cleaned off the food.

WHERE CAN I BUY KEFIR GRAINS AND WATER KEFIR GRAINS?

Kefir grains are available to buy online from sites such as www .kombuchakamp.com. However, getting some surplus from a seasoned brewer who is bound to have an abundance is a much nicer way of sharing. Try sites like kefirhood.com or link up with fermentation groups on social media.

HOW DO YOU FEED KEFIR GRAINS?

Kefir grains come in two different forms: milk kefir and water kefir. Milk kefir looks like clumps of cauliflower, whereas water kefir is more like little crystals. Milk kefir feeds on milk (see page 134) and water kefir feeds on sugary water (see page 280).

HOW LONG WILL KEFIR GRAINS LAST?

If you take good care of your grains by giving them regular and adequate feeds, they will last indefinitely.

WHAT'S A SCOBY AND WHERE CAN I GET ONE?

A scoby is an acronym that stands for symbiotic colony of bacteria and yeast. Although its appearance may challenge some, it's nothing to be scared of. While the term is used specifically when referring to kombucha, kefir grains can also be considered to be a scoby. At The Cultured Club we give all attendees a scoby to take home, but they are also available to buy online from www.kombuchakamp.com or via sharing website such as kefirhood.com, which are springing up as fermentation fever takes hold.

HOW IS A JUN SCOBY DIFFERENT FROM A KOMBUCHA SCOBY?
Although similar in appearance to a kombucha scoby, a jun scoby feeds exclusively off green tea and raw honey. It produces a milder drink that has been referred to as "Champagne kombucha."

MY FERMENT LOOKS OR SMELLS A LITTLE OFF. CAN I STILL EAT IT?
We intrinsically know when something is off, but this can be challenging when you first start making and eating fermented foods, as things smell a little different from what you are used to. However, they taste a lot different to how they smell. It will be fairly obvious if something is harboring a sinister bacteria or mold, but if you want to be surer than sure, buy a pH reader. Sauerkraut is an acidic food, so when it's finished it has a pH of 4.6 or lower. This acidic environment will not permit the growth any bad bacteria, so you can rest assured. To clarify the term "acidic," fermented foods are not acid-causing in the body. In fact, like a lemon, they have an alkalizing effect. They are safe and healthy—what's not to like?

SAUERKRAUTS

IT'S ALWAYS BEST to start with the most well-known ferment. I'm pretty sure that although I had never tasted this fine food or even seen a jar of it, it had filtered into my consciousness. It's not part of my heritage, but its strong hold in certain cultures found its way to my attention from an early age.

Sauerkraut, meaning sour cabbage, is a long way from the boiled cabbages traditionally served in Irish cuisine. Instead of cooking the goodness out of the raw food, the process of fermentation increases the bioavailability of the nutrients, making sauerkraut even more nutritious than the original cabbage. It's low in calories and high in calcium and magnesium, and it's a very good source of dietary fiber, folate, iron, potassium, copper, and manganese.

Sauerkrauts are at their best when they're unpasteurized and uncooked, and the flavor combinations are endless.

Fermented foods provide probiotics and nutrients, but when it comes to fermented cruciferous vegetables like sauerkraut, moderation is the key. It's best to eat fermented cruciferous vegetables as condiments, not as large components of the diet. Many recipes you may see will include the use of whey, and indeed, some recipes in this book do. However, it's not necessary for such things as krauts and other vegetable ferments, as it starts to favor the dominance of whey-type bacteria in your foods. While this isn't a bad thing, we are after variety. We can get our whey bacteria from our kefir and the vegetables can produce their own!

CLASSIC SAUERKRAUT

The simplest sauerkraut you can make is this classic kraut using a process called dry salting, were you mix salt with sliced or grated vegetables to draw their liquid out so that they create their own brine. Use kitchen scales to begin with to help you understand the correct guideline ratios of salt needed per weight of vegetables. Generally you're aiming for a total weight of 1³/₄ pounds of cabbage (vegetables) per one tablespoon of salt. **MAKES 1 X ¹/₂-GALLON JAR**

2 heads of red or white cabbage (or a mix of both)
....
2 tablespoons sea salt
....
I¹/₂ tablespoons juniper berries
....
I tablespoon caraway seeds

1 Remove the outer leaves of the cabbage and cut out the core, then shred the cabbage. I like to shred it reasonably fine. Use your food processor for this if you have one.

2 Place the shredded cabbage in a large bowl and add the salt, giving it a quick massage through the cabbage. Let it sit for 30 to 60 minutes, until it starts to sweat. Mix in the juniper berries and caraway seeds. It should be quite wet now.

3 Begin to fill your clean ¹/₂-gallon jar or crock, taking a handful of cabbage at a time and pressing down very hard using your fist. With each handful you'll notice a little more liquid seeping out.

4 Keep filling the jar until you have filled it to within 1 inch of the top of the jar. For successful fermentation it's crucial to keep the cabbage submerged, so place a weight on it.

5 Leave to sit for anything from one to six weeks. Taste it every few days to gauge the progress of the fermentation flavor. If you're fermenting in an airtight jar, you will also need to "burp" the jar every few days to release the build-up of carbon dioxide.

6 When you're happy with the flavor and texture, store the jar in the fridge. The times will vary with room temperature and other factors. After a week the good bacteria are considered established and it's good to eat, but if you want the maximum probiotics in your sauerkraut, you'll want to let your sauerkraut ferment for up to six weeks.

WHOLE FERMENTED CABBAGE

Throughout Eastern Europe, fermented cabbage leaves are used to make a traditional dish called sarma—or golabki in Polish, golubtsy in Russian, malfoof in Arabic, krautwickel in German, or töltött káposzta in Hungarian. It's a word of Turkish origin meaning food wrapped in leaves, just in case you're wondering! **MAKES 1 X ½-GALLON JAR**

I pointed cabbage

About 3 tablespoons sea salt

Filtered water

1 Remove the core of the cabbage and fill the space where the core was with salt (this is generally about three tablespoons of salt, but you might need a little more or less).

2 Place the cabbage in a clean ½-gallon jar. Pointed cabbages are rather small so they fit nicely in a jar, but it may be necessary to gently peel off some of the loose outer leaves. If that's the case, place them in the bottom of the jar as you do so. Once you have jarred your cabbage, fill the jar with filtered water to within 1 inch of the rim.

3 Allow to ferment for two months at room temperature, until it's soft and tart, then transfer to the fridge and store for up to six months. These leaves can then be chopped into a dinner salad or used to make the stuffed cabbage rolls on page 217.

Spring/summer krauts

Generally when I'm making a kraut, it reflects the season and what I might have around me. You can have so much fun with a kraut, and it's certainly a great way to give life to that lonely carrot or wrinkly beet at the bottom of your vegetable drawer.

Eating foods produced in season is a perfect match for our nutritional needs at that given time of year. Ideally in spring and summer we are eating fresh foods to benefit from all their raw goodness, usually in salads, but I miss the zing that fermentation offers. As an added bonus, by fermenting such nutrient-dense foods, we make them even more nutritious. While fermenting in spring or summer is not a necessity for preservation, it has developed into a year-round must-have for me.

All the following recipes make a 1-quart jar. Follow the method for the classic kraut on page 30 in each case, adding all the ingredients to a large bowl with the salt at the same time.

APPLE GINGER KRAUT WITH ORANGE

This snappy, cheery, light little kraut is a perfect transition from winter to spring and makes a spring plate jump.

I head of red cabbage, shredded

2 green apples, cored and thinly sliced

I orange, unpeeled and sliced into rounds

2-inch piece of fresh ginger, peeled and grated

I tablespoon sea salt

GOLDEN KRAUT

There is a certain joy in packing lots of bright orange foods into a jar. It's as if you're preserving the sun's warmth for colder days ahead.

I small head of green cabbage, shredded

I carrot, grated

I golden beet, peeled and grated

$^1/_2$ apple, grated

I small sweet potato, grated

2-inch piece of fresh ginger, peeled and grated

Handful of fresh cilantro

Orange slices, to decorate

BEET AND KOHLRABI VEGGIE SURPRISE SAUERKRAUT

Kohlrabi is light, like a broccoli stem, while the beets are earthy and deep, so they balance well. They are beautiful raw, but for variety or when a seasonal abundance needs to be preserved, this kraut comes in handy.

$^1/_2$ head of green cabbage, shredded

4 large carrots, grated

I large beet, peeled and chopped

I leek, chopped

I large kohlrabi, peeled and chopped

2 to 3 garlic cloves, chopped

I-inch piece of fresh ginger, peeled and minced

I tablespoon sea salt (check the overall weight of the ingredients—use I tablespoon salt per $1^3/_4$ pounds of vegetables)

HOLA CURTIDO

Curtido is the Central American sauerkraut—and you thought sauerkraut was just a Germanic thing! It's light and fresh with a chili hit.

I head of green cabbage, shredded

I medium onion, thinly sliced

I large or 2 medium carrots, grated

2 jalapeño peppers, deseeded and diced

3 to 4 sprigs of fresh oregano or I tablespoon dried oregano

I sprig of fresh marjoram

$1^1/_2$ tablespoons sea salt

KRISHNA KRAUT

SUPER SPICY SEAWEED KRAUT

APPLE GINGER KRAUT WITH ORANGE

GOLDEN KRAUT

SUPER HULK KRAUT

Put the word hulk *in anything and you are sure to convince your young boys to eat it. This kraut is loaded with the vibrant green goodness of spring and summer to give you all the strength you'll need. It's a wonderful way to take a break from all that wilted kale, plus fermenting it makes all that dietary fiber easier to digest.* **MAKES 1 X 1-QUART JAR**

$\frac{1}{2}$ head of green cabbage, shredded

2 kale stalks, tough stems removed and leaves thinly sliced

I green apple, grated

I carrot, grated

$\frac{1}{2}$ pound daikon radish, grated

Handful of fresh parsley and mint, chopped

I tablespoon sea salt

I teaspoon spirulina powder

Follow the method for the classic sauerkraut on page 30, adding all the ingredients in a large bowl with the salt at the same time.

Autumn/winter krauts

Increasing your intake of fermented foods is great for your gut health. Each mouthful can provide trillions of beneficial bacteria. Allowing these good bacteria to flourish creates a powerful ally for our immune system, 80 percent of which is in our gut. An abundant ecosystem is crucial to deal with the constant pressure our gut bacteria is under every day. In the autumn and winter months I often use my kraut-making as an opportunity to load up on immune-boosting additions such as garlic, ginger, leafy greens, and some spice.

Again, follow the method for the classic sauerkraut on page 30, adding all the ingredients to a large bowl with the salt at the same time. The following five recipes all a make 1-quart jar.

SUPER SPICY SEAWEED KRAUT

Seaweed is an all-round tonic that's great for digestive health. It's high in nutrients and low in calories—everyone's favorite combination!—and it's free for the taking right on our shores. With various authors extolling its virtues, from Prannie Rhatigan to Sally McKenna, we would be foolish not to include it in a kraut.

1 medium head of green cabbage, shredded

1 tablespoon minced fresh ginger

1 tablespoon minced fresh dill

1 tablespoon milled dried seaweed, such as wakame, dulse, or nori

1 tablespoon sea salt

1 teaspoon wasabi powder

1 teaspoon chlorella powder

1 teaspoon spirulina powder

MOROCCAN KRAUT

Adding spices to cabbage, in all their wonderful combinations, continues to surprise me.

1 small red cabbage, shredded

2 carrots, grated

1 preserved lemon (page 97), finely chopped, or 2 to 3 tablespoons lemon juice

2 tablespoons Himalayan salt

1 teaspoon ground ginger or 1 x 1-inch piece of fresh ginger, peeled and grated

1 teaspoon ground cinnamon

1 teaspoon ground turmeric

1 teaspoon ground cumin

$^1/_4$ teaspoon saffron dissolved in a little hot filtered water

FOUR THIEVES KRAUT

As the legend goes, a band of thieves stole from the dead and dying victims of the bubonic plague, but oddly, they were never infected because they used a concoction of herbal oils, now known as Four Thieves Oil, to boost their immunity and protect themselves. Apparently the recipe we share today was given in exchange for a lighter punishment. Whether or not any of this is true, the aromatic herbs in this blend create the illusion of immediate immunity and strength. They are known to stimulate the circulatory, respiratory, and immune systems, and the sauerkraut tastes all the better for it.

I head of green cabbage, shredded

I tablespoon sea salt

$^1/_2$ tablespoon minced fresh rosemary

$^1/_2$ tablespoon minced fresh thyme

$^1/_2$ tablespoon minced fresh sage

$^1/_2$ tablespoon dried lavender

KRISHNA KRAUT

The satisfying warmth, flavor, and spice of Indian food cannot be denied. Preserving it in a jar creates this and more with a subtle citrus undertone. The freshness of flavor is a surprise to the palate as curry takes on a new dimension.

I head of green cabbage, shredded

I$^1/_2$ tablespoons sea salt

$^3/_4$ teaspoon fenugreek

$^3/_4$ teaspoon ground cardamom or fresh seeds (not the whole pods)

$^3/_4$ teaspoon ground turmeric

$^1/_2$ teaspoon mustard seeds

$^1/_2$ teaspoon fennel seeds

$^1/_2$ teaspoon ground ginger or minced fresh ginger

$^1/_2$ teaspoon ground coriander

$^1/_2$ teaspoon paprika

$^1/_2$ teaspoon freshly ground black pepper

CHRISTMAS KRAUT

The traditionalists are rather upset with me for messing with the beloved sauerkraut, but this is every Christmas flavor in a jar. It makes sense of the post-holiday feasting.

I head of red cabbage, shredded

I pound fresh cranberries

Zest and juice of 3 mandarin oranges

Zest of I lemon and juice of $^1/_2$ lemon

2-inch piece of fresh ginger, peeled and grated

$^1/_2$ cup raw cane sugar or coconut sugar

2 tablespoons unrefined sea salt

I teaspoon ground cinnamon or 4 cinnamon sticks

KIMCHI

AS KOREA'S NATIONAL DISH, this ferment really needs its own book (though I'm sure there are a few!), as there are hundreds of traditional varieties. In 2013, UNESCO put kimchi on their Representative List of the Intangible Cultural Heritage of Humanity, so it's here to stay.

There are many kimchi-flavored things, like noodles, but don't let this distract you. The real kimchi is alive, and has a gentle kick and a serious tendency to cause an initial addiction (or repulsion, depending on whether or not your taste buds are ready for the awakening!). It's a complete taste, which just begs for you to eat more—or at least that has been my experience.

The challenge for the novice fermenter is getting past the pungent smell once you open the jar. I blame the garlic. If you aren't used to the smell of fermented garlic, it can throw you for a loop. Watch out, pregnant ladies—I imagine you'll even be able to smell it through the jar!

Kimchi will shake up your plate and add a zing with its complete flavor profile. If it's too much, though, you can balance the flavor with some fresh ingredients and use it as a dressing to smooth out the taste. It would complete a raw plate of crisp lettuce, some sliced raw radishes, and some julienned carrots smothered in kimchi goodness. To make a dressing, simply pulse about 1/2 cup of drained kimchi in a small food processor until you have a coarse puree. Transfer it to a bowl and mix in one tablespoon of sesame oil and three tablespoons of a neutral oil such as mild olive oil or grapeseed oil.

SIMPLE CLASSIC KIMCHI

Mastering a simple classic kimchi will give you the confidence to experiment with more options. **MAKES 1 X 1-QUART JAR**

I x 2¼-pound head of Napa cabbage, chopped or shredded
4 tablespoons sea salt
½ pound daikon (Korean radish), peeled and julienned
4 spring onions, trimmed and cut into I-inch pieces
3 carrots, julienned

FOR THE PASTE:

2 to 3 tablespoons fish sauce (or ¼ teaspoon kelp powder for a vegan option)
5 to 6 garlic cloves, peeled
I-inch piece of fresh ginger, peeled
I to 5 tablespoons Korean red pepper powder (gochugaru), depending on the desired level of heat
A splash of filtered water for blending

1 Remove the outer leaves of the cabbage it they are looking a bit grim. If they look good, wash them well to make sure there is no soil.

2 Chop the cabbage however you like—it really is chopper's choice with this one! Place the chopped cabbage in a large bowl and add the salt, giving it a quick massage through the cabbage until it starts to soften a bit, then add just enough water to cover the cabbage. Put a plate on top and weigh it down with something heavy, leaving it for one hour to kill off any potentially harmful bacteria. Rinse the cabbage thoroughly under cold running water and drain in a colander.

3 While the cabbage drains, make your paste by placing the fish sauce, garlic, and ginger in a blender and blitzing to form a smooth paste, then mix in the gochugaru (one tablespoon for mild and up to five tablespoons for spicy). Add a splash of water if necessary to help it blend.

4 Gently squeeze out any remaining water from the cabbage and return it to the bowl. Add the daikon, spring onions, and carrots, then mix the paste into the vegetables until they are thoroughly coated.

5 Pack the kimchi into a 1-quart jar, pressing down every handful until the brine rises to cover the vegetables, leaving 1 inch of headspace. Add your desired weight (see pages 21–23 for ideas) and seal the jar.

6 Let it ferment for five days. The brine usually escapes, so it's best to place the jar in a bowl or on a plate to catch any overflow. Fermentation is complete after five days. If the taste is to your liking, transfer the jar to the refrigerator. The flavor will deepen and you can eat it until the jar is empty!

7 Following the same technique as outlined above, you can experiment with different vegetables like bok choy, Brussels sprouts (see overleaf), daikon, or cucumber.

BRUSSELS SPROUT KIMCHI

While this might be pushing some of you away at this stage, hear my words of encouragement: this works! I must confess, though, that the first time I made this I did doubt myself, as the smell of the transformed sprouts nearly ruined Christmas. But if anything, kimchi Brussels sprouts could turn a previous sprout hater into a fan. **MAKES 1 X 1-QUART JAR**

Follow the instructions as for the basic kimchi on pages 42–43, simply replacing the cabbage with the same weight of sprouts. Quarter the sprouts or shred them in a food processor for ease of fermenting.

DAIKON RADISH KIMCHI (KKAKDUGI)

Daikon was a relatively unknown vegetable to me until I started making kimchi. Like many vegetables, really, fermentation gives you a deeper reason to get acquainted. Daikon radish kimchi even has its own name. If you're ever in Korea and need a fix, just yell, "Kkakdugi!"

This beautiful root can grow to significant lengths, and this recipe calls for a large one—that would mean about 1 foot long and 3 inches thick. It pretty much follows the same kimchi rules, but with a few additions.

MAKES 1 X 1-QUART JAR

1 large daikon radish (2 pounds)

4 cups filtered water

3 tablespoons sea salt

4 spring onions, cut into ½-inch pieces

FOR THE PASTE:

4 to 6 garlic cloves, peeled

2-inch piece of fresh ginger, peeled

1 to 5 tablespoons Korean red pepper powder (gochugaru), depending on the desired level of heat

1 tablespoon fish sauce (or ¼ teaspoon kelp powder for a vegan option)

1 Cut the greens off the top of the radish and peel the outer layer. (You can use the peppery greens for another purpose—some say they are possibly the best part of this vegetable. Try them in a salad or make them into a pesto.) Cut the radish into 1-inch cubes or slice into rings. Dissolve the salt in the water in a large bowl and add the radish cubes to the brine. Leave to soak for up to six hours.

2 Drain the radish in a colander, reserving 1¾ cups of the brine when draining. Place the radish in a large mixing bowl with the spring onions.

3 Blend the garlic, ginger, red pepper powder, and fish sauce together in a blender or food processor until it forms a paste. Mix in with the radish and spring onions until the vegetables are nicely coated with the paste.

4 Ferment as outlined on page 43, but note that the radish will take at least two weeks to ferment because it's a bit larger than other kimchi creations.

CUCUMBER KIMCHI (OI-SOBAGI)

Kimchi is so good that the variations are plentiful, all with their own name. This one is oi-sobagi. ***MAKES 1 X 1-QUART JAR***

2 long, thin-skinned cucumbers

2 tablespoons sea salt

FOR THE PASTE:

I cup filtered water

2 tablespoons rice flour

I bunch of spring onions

3 garlic cloves

75g Korean red pepper powder (gochugaru)

I teaspoon sea salt

I large carrot, cut into long, thin strips with a vegetable peeler

1 Cut the cucumbers horizontally into 3- to 4-inch sections, then slice each section vertically in a cross but leave it attached at the bottom. Place the cucumbers in a colander set over a large bowl, then salt them generously, rubbing salt over all the cut surfaces but trying not to break them apart. Place the cucumbers in the colander cut end down and allow them to drain into the bowl (reserve the drained liquid) for about 45 minutes, until soft.

2 While the cucumbers are draining, make the paste. This is slightly different from the other recipes, as the paste will be thicker, for stuffing. Place the water and rice flour into a pot set over a low heat and stir constantly for three to four minutes, until thickened. Remove from the heat and allow to cool to room temperature. Blend the spring onions and garlic in a food processor.

3 After the cucumbers have had their time, give them a gentle squeeze over the colander. Pour this liquid into the rice paste in the pot and stir to combine. Stir in the gochugaru and salt and mix to combine, then add the carrot ribbons.

4 Give the cucumbers a quick rinse to remove any excess salt, then pat them dry with a tea towel and rub the paste over all the surfaces of the cucumbers. Stuff some in and close the cucumber as much as possible. Repeat with all the cucumber pieces.

5 Pack the stuffed cucumbers into a clean 1-quart jar as tightly as possible, allowing the paste to settle into all the gaps. Place your chosen weight in (see pages 21–23 for ideas) for successful fermentation, making sure you leave 1 inch of headspace at the top of the jar. Cover with a fitted lid and let it sit at room temperature for one to two days. The paste will become more liquid—this is normal.

6 Cucumber will turn to mush relatively quickly, so to enjoy this at its prime; eat within three to four days of fermenting.

SWEET RICE PASTE

If you would like to use a thicker, more substantial paste for your kimchi experiments, this rice paste is worth the effort.

¹/₄ pound spring onions

I cup filtered water

2 tablespoons sweet rice flour

2 to 3 garlic cloves, peeled

I-inch piece of fresh ginger, peeled

2 to 4 tablespoons Korean red pepper powder (gochugaru), depending on the desired level of heat

I tablespoon superfine sugar

I tablespoon fish sauce (or ¹/₄ teaspoon kelp powder for a vegan option)

1 Cut the roots off the spring onions and remove any bad parts, then wash them well.

2 To make a sweet rice paste for kimchi, combine the water and sweet rice flour in a small pot, mixing well. Cook on a medium-high heat, stirring, until it starts to bubble. Turn off the heat and let it cool down.

3 Once cool, blend with the other ingredients in a blender or food processor to form a smooth paste.

VEGETABLE FERMENTS

A GENEROUS PORTION of our diets should be fresh vegetables and ideally we should enjoy them raw to experience their full flavor. This is clearly more achievable in the summer months and is only really applicable if you are buying organic, preferably from a local producer. Taste and quality diminish drastically the farther away you get from the farm.

In Northern Ireland, I'm very fortunate to live near Helen's Bay Organic Gardens, where delicious vegetables are not only grown without chemicals, but also from their own vegan-friendly compost of grass, straw, seaweed, and the minimal farm waste. John McCormick, who established the gardens, has a particular commitment to soil, sustainability, and quality, and although he has an extensive CSA program and loyal market stall customers, there is always a seasonal glut of produce that will make its way into the jar. This closes the loop for food waste and enables the beautiful quality of his produce to be preserved and augmented.

Fermenting your vegetables elevates them from ordinary food to superfood. They become alive with probiotics, enzymes, vitamins, and minerals, and are much easier to digest, which is a boost for more compromised systems. Plus they're exceptionally easy to prepare. And if you want to speed up the vegetable fermentation process, try using a starter liquid, which inoculates the food with good bacteria. Options include:

- **Brine from a previous ferment:** The fermented vegetable juice from a previous batch can be added to a new batch as a starter. Add about $1/4$ cup brine per quart of vegetables.
- **Other fermented liquids:** Unflavored water, kefir, or kombucha can be used as a starter culture for fermenting vegetables. Add $1/4$ cup per quart of vegetables.
- **Whey strained from milk kefir:** Again, add $1/4$ cup per quart of vegetables.

Seeds (legumes)

Apart from sweet corn, seeds grow in pods that are sometimes eaten along with the seed, e.g. beans (green beans, French beans, butterbeans, snake beans), broad beans, peas, and snow peas.

DILLY BEANS

I always have a few jars of these on hand, as they are the perfect snack for both adults and children. They do a great job at killing a sugar craving and stop you from reaching for a carbohydrate substitute. Thankfully, it's one ferment my kids will eat straight out of the jar.

MAKES 1 X 1-QUART JAR

1³/₄ pound green beans (enough to tightly pack your jar)

I small bunch of fresh dill

3 garlic cloves

¹/₄ jalapeño pepper (optional)

I teaspoon celery seeds

2 percent brine solution (I tablespoon sea salt dissolved in 4 cups filtered water)

1 Chop off the tough bits at the ends of the beans and the rough ends of the stalks of dill.

2 Put the garlic in the bottom of your clean 1-quart jar, then pack half the beans into the jar, standing upright. Put the dill and the jalapeño pepper, if using, in the middle of the jar, then fill in the outside edges with the rest of the beans. Add the celery seeds and shake them around the jar, then pour in enough brine to cover the veggies, leaving a 1-inch gap at the top. Keep the veggies submerged, but I find the beans don't need the addition of a weight if you have packed them in tightly enough.

3 Leave in a cool, dark place for one to three weeks. When the beans have reached your desired flavor, texture, and acidity, they are ready to eat. Once open, store in the fridge for up to six months.

DILLY BEANS

SWEET AND SOUR SUGAR SNAP PEAS

SWEET AND SOUR SUGAR SNAP PEAS

These peas make a great probiotic side dish or a crispy snack. I appreciate that they are sweet and delicious when raw or lightly steamed, but when they are fermented they take on a whole new personality.

Once your peas are all gone, don't throw out that brine and the remaining spices. Rather, prepare some more veggies (such as peas, onions, zucchini, or cucumber slices), pack them into a clean jar with some fresh spices, pour the brine over them, and ferment again! See page 91 for more uses for brine.

MAKES 1 X 1-QUART JAR

¹/₂ cup raw mild honey

²/₃ cup raw apple cider vinegar

I tablespoon sea salt

I tablespoon pickling spice

I teaspoon mustard powder

I teaspoon pink peppercorns (optional)

2¹/₄ pounds sugar snap peas

I celery stalk or a generous pinch of celery seeds

3 medium garlic cloves, smashed

Filtered water to top up if necessary

1 In a medium bowl, combine the honey, vinegar, salt, pickling spice, mustard, and celery seeds (if using). Stir well to dissolve the honey and salt. You may need to let this sit for an hour or two to get everything to dissolve and combine well.

2 Wash the peas and celery stalk thoroughly. Remove and discard the ends from the peas.

3 Pack the peas, celery, and garlic into a clean 1-quart jar. Pour the honey and vinegar mixture over the veggies. Pack down the veggies so that they are completely covered by the liquid, topping up with filtered water if necessary. Leave 1 inch of headspace at the top of the jar. The peas will float up to the top, so you need to weigh them down for successful fermentation.

4 Put a lid on the jar and leave at room temperature for two days, then transfer to the refrigerator. They will keep well for at least two months, after which time they will begin to lose their crunch.

NASTURTIUM CAPERS

Come the late summer, all those vibrant, peppery nasturtium flowers will start to form seedpods. They grow in a cluster of three, but easily separate out into individual nuggets ready to be transformed into little bursts of peppery tang. Nasturtium capers are traditionally called poor man's capers. When fermented, the seeds soften and have a similar taste profile to capers. Pick them when green and soft for the best results. **MAKES 1 X ¹/₂-PINT JAR**

Enough nasturtium seedpods to fill a ¹/₂-pint jar

2 percent brine solution (I tablespoon sea salt dissolved in 4 cups filtered water)

CHOOSE ONE OR TWO FROM THE FOLLOWING OR USE YOUR OWN FAVORITE FLAVORS:

¹/₄ teaspoon fennel seeds

¹/₄ teaspoon coriander seeds

¹/₄ teaspoon peppercorns

Garlic cloves

Chilies

Fresh tarragon

Fresh cilantro

Fresh thyme

Fresh rosemary

Bay leaves

1 Split the seedpod clusters into single seeds and wash and dry them if they need it, then place in a clean ¹/₂-pint jar along with your flavorings and cover with the 2 percent brine solution. Use a weight to keep them submerged, as they will want to bob up. Leave 1 inch of headspace at the top of the jar.

2 Leave to ferment for at least one month, then store for up to six months in the fridge.

Root vegetables

Usually a long or round-shaped taproot, such as beet, carrot, celeriac, daikon, parsnip, radish, rutabaga, and turnip. All will work wonderfully well as a fermented food.

DILLY CARROTS TWO WAYS

Dilly carrots are fresh and fragrant and you won't be disappointed if you give this recipe a go. You can use grated carrots or carrot sticks, but lacto-fermented carrot sticks are an easy side dish to add probiotics to any meal or snack. While grating carrots is a brilliant option (either by hand or in a food processor), I like to spiralize carrots for the extra fun of it. A mandoline is another wonderful kitchen gadget that will allow you to julienne them, which will give a fuller, crispier texture to the finished ferment.

DILLY CARROTS

CARROT STICKS

#1 DILLY CARROTS

MAKES 1 X 1-QUART JAR

2¼ pounds carrots—the bigger, the better for processing

I bunch of fresh dill

I tablespoon sea salt

1 Process the carrots however you like, either using a food processor, mandoline, spiralizer, or grater. Remove the stems from the dill and chop the fronds finely for an even mix.

2 Place the carrots and dill in a bowl. Sprinkle the sea salt and massage it through the vegetables until they feel wet.

3 Pack the mixture into a clean 1-quart flip-top jar, pressing each handful down tightly to ensure no air is trapped. Pack the jar tightly, leaving 1 inch headspace at the top of the jar. Make sure the carrots and dill are completely submerged under the liquid that has been released.

4 Close the lid and allow to ferment for five days at room temperature, then store the jar in the fridge for up to six months. Carrots are best enjoyed within this time, as they tend to get mushy after six months.

#2 CARROT STICKS

MAKES 1 X 1-QUART JAR

6 carrots, unpeeled and cut into sticks

I to 2 garlic cloves, smashed

I tablespoon chopped fresh dill

2 percent brine solution (I tablespoon sea salt dissolved in 4 cups filtered water)

1 Place the carrots, smashed garlic cloves, and fresh dill into a clean 1-quart jar. Packing them vertically is the most efficient way to get a tight pack in the jar. Cover with the 2 percent brine to within 1 inch of the top of the jar.

2 Leave to ferment on the countertop for at least two weeks. Taste after this time and continue to ferment until you have achieved your desired flavor. Once you are happy with the taste and texture, you can dig in. Store in the fridge for up to six months once opened.

MOROCCAN CARROTS

Carrots leave a lot of room for playing with flavor. It's one of the beauties of fermentation, so let your culinary curiosity guide you. Moroccan carrots are a wonderful variation. **MAKES 1 X 1-QUART JAR**

2¹/₄ pounds carrots, peeled and grated

2 garlic cloves, minced

I small bunch of fresh cilantro, chopped

I tablespoon lemon juice

I teaspoon ground cumin

¹/₂ teaspoon ground cinnamon

2 teaspoons sea salt

Prepare as for the dilly carrots #1 on page 58.

CARROTS WITH AN INDIAN TWIST

Indian spice is tasty with most things. Leftover paste from making the hot chili sauce on page 118 is perfect in place of the chili flakes here. **MAKES 1 X 1-QUART JAR**

2¹/₄ pounds carrots, peeled and grated

I knob of fresh ginger, peeled and grated

2 teaspoons chili flakes

2 teaspoons fenugreek

2 teaspoons mustard seed

I teaspoon ground turmeric

I tablespoon sea salt

Prepare as for the dilly carrots #1 on page 58.

PINK PICKLED TURNIPS #1

Turnips appear on the plates of many dishes, from the Middle East to Japan. Fermented turnips even have their own name, sauerruben, which means "sour turnip." There was a time I couldn't imagine anything worse, turnip being my number one most disliked vegetable. Now, though, I'm at peace with this humble vegetable. Beet is used to influence the color and seaweed is added for that Japanese twist. This recipe also works well with rutabaga. **MAKES 2 X 1-QUART JARS**

10 small turnips, peeled
....
I small beet, peeled and thickly sliced
....
3 garlic cloves, smashed
....
I piece of kombu seaweed
....
2 percent brine solution (2 tablespoons sea salt dissolved in 8 cups filtered water)

1 Place the whole small turnips, sliced beets, garlic, and seaweed in two clean 1-quart jars, then pour the brine over the vegetables. Gently press down on the vegetables to release any air bubbles and to submerge them in the brine.

2 Cover the jar with a lid, then place the jar on a plate to catch any overflow that may happen once the active fermentation gets going.

3 Leave the jars at room temperature for five days. You should start to see some bubbles on top, which is a sign that fermentation is underway. After this time, the turnips should have a clean, lightly sour smell and taste. As they are a solid vegetable, I like to leave them out for a lot longer—up to three or four weeks—to develop even more flavor and to soften a little. Once you're happy with the taste, put the jars in the fridge. Lacto-fermented turnips will keep in the refrigerator for at least six months, but are best eaten within three months, as after that time they tend to lose some of their crispness.

PINK PICKLED TURNIPS #2

If waiting for months on end before you can break into that jar of sour turnips seems like torture, then preparing them as detailed below will speed things along. **MAKES 1 X 1-QUART JAR**

I³/₄ pounds turnips, peeled and spiralized, sliced into sticks, or any other way you prefer
....
¹/₂ small beet, peeled and sliced
....
I garlic clove, thinly sliced
....
I bay leaf
....
A few sprigs of fresh dill
....
Pinch of chili flakes (optional)
....
¹/₂ cup raw apple cider vinegar (optional)
....
2 percent brine solution (I tablespoon sea salt dissolved in 4 cups filtered water)

1 Place the turnips, beet, garlic, bay leaf, dill, and chili flakes, if using, into a clean 1-quart jar. Add the vinegar, then pour the brine over the vegetables, making sure you leave 1 inch of headspace at the top of the jar.

2 Cover the jar and let it sit at room temperature to pickle for one week. Refrigerate until ready to serve and use within one month.

GINGER

To use this ferment, don't cook it—you should only use it raw. You can have a slice or two with a dish or you can chop it up and mix it into any dish that calls for ginger by adding it at the end. **MAKES 1 X ¹/₂-PINT JAR**

Juice of 5 lemons

I tablespoon sea salt

I teaspoon ground turmeric

I pound fresh ginger, peeled and very thinly sliced (enough to fill a ¹/₂-pint jar)

1 Mix the lemon juice, salt, and turmeric together in a jug, stirring to dissolve the salt. Pack the thinly sliced ginger into a clean ¹/₂-pint jar and pour the liquid over the contents. You will need to weigh it down for a successful ferment. Leave 1 inch of headspace at the top of the jar.

2 Close the lid and allow to ferment on your countertop at room temperature for two weeks. Once it's ready, transfer to the fridge, where it will keep for at least six months.

HORSERADISH

This amazing vegetable is low in calories but rich in antioxidants, minerals, vitamins, and dietary fiber. It's also effective in killing off many different parasites and bacteria that cause dysentery, salmonella, and tuberculosis. In addition, it stimulates the pancreatic enzymes and intestinal juices, which in turn improves the function of the digestive system. Its root is beneficial for your heart, circulation, and liver, and it helps to alleviate rheumatism, as it acts as a potent diuretic. But that's not all! Horseradish can help in the treatment of the flu, respiratory disorders, tonsillitis, and urinary tract infections too.

However, like all things worthy, there's a catch. Unless you're an avid forager it's hard to get, so you'll need to make a special request at the market for it. And when you finally have it in your possession, it's a potent root to work with. Your eyes will sting, so defend them by wearing whatever protective gear you can: sunglasses, swimming goggles, or safety glasses will all help. **MAKES 1 X 1/2-PINT JAR**

1/2 pound fresh horseradish root, peeled

2 percent brine solution (1 tablespoon sea salt dissolved in 4 cups filtered water)

1 Prepare yourself for the burn of the volatile oils of the horseradish by wearing eye protection! Shred the horseradish in a food processor with the grating attachment or use a box grater. If you're using a food processor, switch to the regular S-blade now.

2 Add the brine to the food processor and blend until a smooth paste forms, adding a little additional water if necessary to help it blend. Take a deep breath and spoon the horseradish paste into a clean 1/2-pint jar, making sure you leave 1 inch of headspace at the top of the jar. Cover with a lid.

3 Allow to ferment for at least three days at room temperature. Once fermented, this will keep in the fridge for several months.

Tubers

Vegetables that grow underground on the root of a plant, such as Jerusalem artichokes, potatoes, sweet potatoes, and yams. If you are into gardening, chances are you have a potato or two growing, possibly even an artichoke, so take note!

FERMENTED MASHED POTATOES

You might be raising an eyebrow as you read this, wondering why you've never heard of fermented potatoes before (besides in poutine) or where this fermenting obsession will end. However, soaking potatoes in a brine overnight prior to simmering, baking, roasting, broiling, or frying them is a traditional food preparation technique that has been forgotten in our modern kitchens.

Fermenting your roots before eating them makes them more digestible and reduces the roots' glucose and fructose content. The starch can be a real pain for those with an imbalanced gut, as it is the perfect food for pathogens. The upside of soaking and fermenting potatoes is that the digested starch won't spike blood sugars.

The best way to ferment potatoes is to use a basic brine. **SERVES 4**

2¼ pounds potatoes, peeled

2 percent brine solution (1 tablespoon sea salt dissolved in 4 cups filtered water)

2 cups milk kefir (page 134)

1 tablespoon sea salt

1 Soak your potatoes for a few hours in a 2 percent brine solution. Pour off the water, then bake or boil the potatoes as per usual. When they are cooked through and tender, mash them in a large clean bowl with the kefir and sea salt. Cover with a clean cotton cloth and secure with a rubber band.

2 Leave the covered bowl on the counter for two days, then refrigerate in an airtight container for up to one month. My favorite way to serve it is to supercharge it with a little grated garlic, a generous glug of olive oil, and a squeeze of lemon juice—a homage to the Greek dish skordalia.

Bulbs

Bulbs usually grow just below the surface of the ground and produce a fleshy, leafy shoot above ground, such as fennel, garlic, leek, onion, shallot, and spring onion.

FENNEL

The beautiful anise flavor of a fennel bulb lends itself to the additional tang of fermentation. You can have a lot of fun with this flavor, pairing it with apple, herbs, orange, cucumber, and all manner of roots and fruits. No doubt your creative culinary juices will start flowing. This recipe will get your taste buds ready. **MAKES 1 X 1-QUART JAR**

2 to 3 fennel bulbs, thinly sliced

3 carrots, peeled and thinly sliced

2 to 3 spring onions or other sweet onion, thinly sliced

I to 2 lemons, thinly sliced

2 garlic cloves, chopped

I tablespoon whole black peppercorns

2 percent brine solution (I tablespoon sea salt dissolved in 4 cups filtered water)

1 Place the fennel, carrots, spring onions, lemon, garlic, and peppercorns in a clean 1-quart jar or crock.

2 Pour the brine over the vegetables, making sure there is enough brine to cover the vegetables by at least 3 inches. Put a weight on top of the vegetables in order to keep them completely submerged, making sure you leave 1 inch of headspace at the top of the jar.

3 Allow to ferment at room temperature for one week, tasting the vegetables periodically as they ferment. When finished, refrigerate for up to four weeks.

ONIONS

This may seem a little radical, but I don't overly peel my onions (or my garlic) when using them in a ferment. Leaving on the onions' outer skin provides an exceptionally rich source of plant compounds called flavonoids, especially the powerful antioxidant and anti-inflammatory compound called quercetin. When I add onion skins to fermented foods, it concentrates the quercetin and hides the bitter taste while tenderizing the tough skin.

Whole fermented onions are a staple in my kitchen. I love having them on hand to serve with omelets, mix into sauces, or blend into dips.

MAKES 1 X 1-QUART JAR

3 large onions (red or white), peeled and halved

About 1 tablespoon sea salt

Filtered water

1 It's easiest to slice the onions in a food processor to save your tears, but if this isn't an option, slice them thinly, chopping from the top to the bottom. Transfer to a bowl and add the salt (use one tablespoon sea salt per $2^1/_4$ pounds onion). Give this a quick massage, but don't get too involved or you'll be a mess with tears. Pack into a clean 1-quart jar and top with enough water to submerge the onions. Place a suitable weight on top, making sure you leave 1 inch of headspace at the top of the jar, and close the jar.

2 Leaving the onions to ferment on the countertop for at least six weeks will result in a ferment that is sweet and soft. Transfer them to your fridge, where they will keep for up to a year.

GARLIC

Having a jar of fermented garlic will become a kitchen staple once you realize how beneficial it is. The cloves and brine are perfect for homemade salad dressings, marinades, or any savory dish that calls for fresh garlic. They add an amazing flavor to cooked dishes and have an even greater nutritional value than fresh garlic. Fermented garlic tastes like a cross between raw and roasted garlic, and the cloves become almost buttery in texture.

Peeling an adequate quantity of cloves isn't much fun, so crank up the music or practice rhythmic breathing, meditation, your pelvic floor exercises, or whatever allows you to complete a mundane task with joy. And I have to warn you that the aroma that seeps out is intensely garlicky, but you'll become immune to it after a while, as will your family, and it's well worth it.

Just remember not to cook the fermented garlic, as it destroys the probiotics and extra vitamins you have created. Use it when making hummus, pestos, and salsas or finely grate it into a salad or at the end of cooking curries for an extra kick. Don't worry, people will still talk to you after you eat it. Fermenting garlic actually helps to calm the common garlic breath associated with eating this wondrous bulb. ***MAKES 1 X 1-QUART JAR***

12 heads of garlic

2 percent brine solution (1 tablespoon sea salt dissolved in 4 cups filtered water)

1 Remove most of the loose skins from the garlic cloves. I generally leave the last layer on, which is always the hardest one to peel. Place the garlic cloves into a clean 1-quart jar. Cover the garlic with the brine, leaving 1 inch of headspace at the top of the jar. Weigh down with whatever weight you have available (see pages 21–23 for ideas).

2 Forget about it for four to six weeks as it ferments away at room temperature. Some cloves may turn blue, but don't be alarmed—it's due to the sulfur compounds. Once fermented, store in the refrigerator for up to a year.

KOREAN-STYLE PICKLED GARLIC

Like all good things, you need to put in a little work to make this worthwhile. While technically this isn't a ferment, it's worth the effort.

MAKES 1 X 1-QUART JAR

8 to 9 heads of garlic, peeled and washed

FOR THE VINEGAR BRINE (STAGE ONE):

1¹/₃ cups filtered water

²/₃ cup rice wine vinegar

1 tablespoon sea salt

FOR THE SOY BRINE (STAGE TWO):

1¹/₃ cups filtered water

²/₃ cup soy sauce

¹/₄ cup rice wine vinegar

3 tablespoons raw cane sugar

1 This pickle is a two-stage process. For the first stage, peel two layers of the skin off the garlic cloves, then wash and drain the garlic in a strainer for two hours. Meanwhile, combine the water, rice wine vinegar, and salt, stirring to dissolve the salt.

2 Place the drained garlic in a clean 1-quart jar. Fill up the jar with the vinegar brine, making sure you leave 1 inch of headspace at the top of the jar.

3 Leave it to ferment for ten days at room temperature. After ten days, drain the vinegar brine from the jar.

4 The second stage is to make the soy brine. Bring all the soy brine ingredients to a boil, then reduce the heat and gently simmer for five minutes over a medium heat. Allow to cool completely. Pour the cooled soy brine over the garlic cloves, making sure all the garlic cloves are completely submerged.

5 Close tightly with a lid and let it ferment at room temperature for three weeks. The garlic can be eaten at this point, but it will continue to taste better as it matures. After opening, store in the refrigerator, where it will keep for a few months.

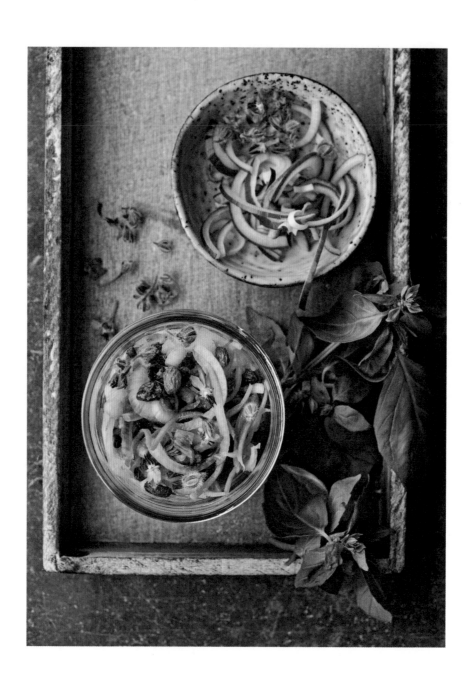

SWEET AND SPICY ONION RELISH

There is no need to buy condiments when you fall in love with the simplicity of fermenting your own. Your pocket will love you, your tummy will love you, and your summer BBQ will never be the same again. **MAKES 1 X 1-QUART JAR**

4 small onions, peeled and halved
....
3 to 4 carrots, peeled and chopped
....
$^2/_3$ cup golden raisins
....
Handful of fresh basil leaves
....
$^1/_2$ teaspoon cumin seeds
....
2 percent brine solution (1 tablespoon sea salt dissolved in 4 cups filtered water)

1 Pulse the onions in a food processor until they are a fine mince. Add the carrots and pulse until fully combined with the onions, but still a little coarse. Place all the remaining ingredients in the processor and blend until it's fine or coarse, depending on your preference.

2 Tightly pack the mixture into a clean 1-quart jar, making sure you leave 1 inch of headspace at the top of the jar. Let it ferment at room temperature for three days, then transfer to the fridge. This will keep for at least six months once opened.

Flowers

The edible flowers of certain vegetables, such as broccoli, cauliflower, choi sum, globe artichokes, or zucchini or other squash flowers, work, brilliantly as ferments.

INDIAN-SPICED LACTO-FERMENTED CAULIFLOWER

In this section we're going crazy and mixing up stems, roots, and bulbs!

I love the fact that even though fermentation clearly has an exact science behind it, the parameters are rather generous, giving you lots of scope for experimentation. I've had lots of fun adding a bit of this and a bit of that, as fermentation feeds right into the philosophy of wasteless creation.

I will admit that using broccoli or cauliflower creates an unbelievably pungent ferment, so save them for later experimentation, when your nostrils and taste buds have become accustomed to the smell and your giddy excitement at trying these out simply cannot be contained any longer. Starting with a variation on a well-known theme, this ferment is a take on the beloved piccalilli. The fragrant blend of spice will mask the pungency of a raw cauliflower ferment. **MAKES 1 X 1-QUART JAR**

I small head of cauliflower, cut into bite-sized pieces

3 garlic cloves, chopped

I tablespoon curry powder

I tablespoon chili powder

I teaspoon ground turmeric

I teaspoon cayenne pepper

2 percent brine solution (I tablespoon sea salt dissolved in 4 cups filtered water)

1 Layer the cauliflower, garlic, and spices in a clean 1-quart jar, gently pressing the cauliflower. Pour in the brine solution to fill up the jar, leaving 1 inch headspace at the top. Cover tightly and shake to disperse the spices and dissolve the salt, then open the jar and put in your weight of choice (see pages 21–23 for ideas).

2 Leave to sit at room temperature for three days. At this stage, you can taste it and leave it out at room temperature for another week to continue to ferment until your desired flavor and texture are reached. Store in the fridge for up to three months.

ZESTY BROCCOLI STEM PICKLES

I prefer to eat my broccoli heads as they are, as fermenting them has ended in disaster. However, the stems make a wonderful ferment. They are crunchy and the perfect pickle texture.

MAKES 1 X 1-QUART JAR

2¹/₄ pounds broccoli (look for bunches with long, thick stems)

....

¹/₂ teaspoon chili flakes

....

2 percent brine solution (1 tablespoon sea salt dissolved in 4 cups filtered water)

1 Peel off the outer layer of the broccoli stems. Chop the stems into sticks and place them upright in a clean 1-quart jar. Sprinkle in the chili flakes and cover them with the 2 percent brine solution. If the stems are tightly packed, there's no need for a weight, but make sure they are submerged—use your judgment. Leave 1 inch of headspace at the top of the jar.

2 Close the lid and leave to ferment at room temperature for at least seven days. Check after this time for your desired flavor and texture, but as this is a quick ferment, by two weeks it will be at the point of being over-fermented. Once you're happy with the ferment, store the pickles in the fridge for up to six months.

Fruits

Vegetable fruit are fleshy and contain seeds, such as chilies, cucumbers, eggplants, melons, peppers, plantains, pumpkin and squash, tomatillos, tomatoes, and zucchini.

BUTTERNUT SQUASH

Serve as a snack or top with some sour cream or mayonnaise for a beautiful salad.

MAKES 1 X 1-QUART JAR

1¹/₂ pounds butternut squash

12 to 15 fresh sage leaves

2 percent brine solution (1 tablespoon sea salt dissolved in 4 cups filtered water)

1 Using a large, sharp knife, cut the stem end and bottom off the squash. Set the squash on a stable cutting board and cut off the outer peel with the knife. Save one piece of the peel to act as a weight. Cut the squash in half and remove the seeds and fibers from the centre, then chop the squash into 1-inch cubes.

2 Place the squash cubes in a clean 1-quart jar. Add the sage and brine and shake to mix. Include the saved piece of peel, placing it on top of the squash to keep the cubes submerged. Leave 1 inch of headspace at the top of the jar and cover with a lid.

3 Allow to ferment for at least one week at room temperature. Ferment longer for softer, stronger-tasting squash, but no longer than three weeks. Transfer to the fridge for up to three months.

ZUCCHINI

Zucchini are the avid gardener's joke and this is yet another variation to add to the list of how to use a zucchini. **MAKES 1 X 1-PINT JAR**

I pound zucchini, sliced into rounds ¼-inch thick
....
I bunch of fresh chives, chopped
....
4 to 8 fresh sage leaves
....
2 to 3 sprigs of fresh rosemary
....
Zest of I lemon
....
I garlic clove, smashed
....
2 percent brine solution (½ tablespoon sea salt dissolved in 2 cups filtered water)
....
2 to 3 clean grape leaves, oak leaves, cherry leaves, raspberry or blackberry leaves, or pomegranate skins (optional)

1 Tightly pack the sliced zucchini, herbs, lemon zest, and garlic clove in a clean pint jar until it's about three-quarters full. Pour the brine into the jar, topping up with additional water if needed. Add in your leaves of choice or the skin of a used pomegranate (this can also double as a weight), if using. You can leave them out, but they make a big difference in how crisp the pickles will be due to the tannin in the leaves, which makes the pickles crunchy. Leave 1 inch of headspace at the top of the jar.

2 Seal the jar and let it sit on the counter for three days, then place in the refrigerator to further culture. The zucchini is ready to eat after about a week, but it will keep fermenting and aging, much like a fine wine. Check it regularly and eat within two to three weeks so that you won't be disappointed by a soggy, neglected ferment.

CUCUMBER PICKLES

If you have friends and family members in doubt, make this sweet little ferment and enjoy watching them dig in. It's similar enough to a common pickle that it shouldn't raise too much suspicion. **MAKES 1 X 1-QUART JAR**

I fresh grape leaf or cherry leaf (optional, but it makes a better ferment)

3¹/₃ pounds pickling cucumbers, thinly sliced

I sweet onion, thinly sliced

I cup fresh lemon juice

I cup raw honey or maple syrup

3 tablespoons unrefined sea salt (or 2 percent of the total weight of the ingredients)

I to 2 tablespoons celery seeds

I tablespoon yellow mustard seeds

2 teaspoons ground turmeric

1 Put the leaf in the bottom of your clean 1-quart jar so that it lies flat. This helps the cucumbers to stay crisp.

2 Toss the cucumber and onion slices together in a large bowl, then transfer to the jar, pressing them down lightly with your fist or a pounder.

3 Combine the remaining ingredients in a jug and pour it over the cucumbers. This should be enough to submerge them in liquid, but if it isn't, top them up with filtered water if necessary to cover. Leave 1 inch of headspace at the top of the jar.

4 Seal the jar and keep at room temperature for about two days. Cucumbers soften easily, so after this time transfer them to the fridge and eat within two to three weeks to avoid mushy disappointment.

JALAPEÑOS

Jalapeños are reported to have various positive health properties, including anti-inflammatory, cancer-fighting, and cardiovascular benefits. They also boost metabolism and provide migraine relief, plus they're really tasty. Fermenting them also takes care of the chili sting if that's a problem for you.

MAKES 1 X 1-QUART JAR

15 to 20 fresh jalapeño peppers

24 garlic cloves, peeled

$^1/_2$ red onion, thinly sliced

4 cups filtered water

3 tablespoons sea salt

1 Wash the jalapeños well. You may want to slit them open or slice them so that the brine and fermentation can happen more readily inside the peppers and not just from the outside. Place the jalapeños, garlic cloves, and sliced onion in a clean 1-quart jar.

2 Mix the water and the salt together, stirring to dissolve the salt. Pour enough of this brine over the vegetables to fully cover them. Place a weight on top to keep them submerged, making sure you leave 1 inch of headspace at the top of the jar.

3 Close the lid and let the jar sit on your counter for several weeks. Move to the fridge for longer-term storage, although these would keep well on the countertop, continuing to ferment, for up to two months. Once they are fermented to taste, transfer them to the fridge, where they'll keep for at least six months. I've even seen chili seeds sprouting in the fermentation brine, illustrating that it truly is a living environment.

TOMATOES

It's only when you're alone in a polytunnel full of tomatoes that you get a sense of how bizarre these plants truly are. While their fruits are to be enjoyed, as a member of the nightshade family, the plant is actually poisonous.

Fermented tomatoes in a brine solution have a special sweet-and-sour tingling taste that bursts in the mouth, especially if you use cherry tomatoes. Eastern Europeans have been preserving tomatoes for centuries in a pickling brine of salt, garlic, and dill. It's a surprising taste, as the tomatoes slightly fizz on the tongue. This sweet and salty taste will go well with mild food and will bring a sense of party to the plate. I've given you an easy recipe to get you started. **MAKES 1 X 1-QUART JAR**

$^3/_4$ pound ripe cherry tomatoes or 10 vine tomatoes

5 garlic cloves, sliced

1 small bunch of fresh dill

1 bay leaf

1 teaspoon whole black peppercorns

2 tablespoons sea salt

2 tablespoons raw cane sugar

4 cups lukewarm filtered water

1 Prick each tomato once with a fork to pierce the skin, then pack the tomatoes fairly tightly into a clean 1-quart jar, distributing the garlic, dill, bay leaf and peppercorns between the tomatoes.

2 Mix the salt and sugar with the lukewarm filtered water, stirring to dissolve. Pour this sweet 4 percent brine into the jar, making sure all the tomatoes are covered. Use a weight to keep them submerged, making sure you leave 1 inch of headspace at the top of the jar.

3 Leave to ferment for three to five days at room temperature, after which time pop them in the fridge, where they'll keep for up to two months.

TOMATO SALSA

The Cultured Club salsa has reached a level of local fame simply because it's so delicious. This salsa is alive—you won't be disappointed. To me, the lively tang of fermentation suggests that this is what salsa should taste like. A huge added bonus is that your efforts in prepping all the ingredients are preserved. For all the times that you have been outcast because of your fermenting addiction, the most unconvinced family member or friend will be pleasantly surprised by this one! **MAKES 1 X 1-QUART JAR**

8 to 10 ripe tomatoes, roughly chopped

2 red or green peppers, roughly chopped

1 medium onion, roughly chopped

1 to 2 garlic cloves, minced

Juice of 1 lime

Handful of fresh cilantro, chopped

2 teaspoons fine sea salt (add more if needed)

$1/2$ teaspoon cumin seeds

$1/2$ teaspoon freshly ground black pepper

Pinch of smoked paprika

1 This is an easy one. Simply mix together all the ingredients in a bowl, then pack into a clean 1-quart jar, making sure you leave 1 inch of headspace at the top of the jar.

2 Close the lid and allow to ferment for at least three days at room temperature. Salsas have always been one of the more lively ferments and it makes a lot of noise. As the carbon dioxide escapes it brings some of that lovely juice with it, so place the jar on a dish to collect the juice and open it with care (although personally, I don't mind being covered in salsa juice).

3 Once it's ready, transfer to the fridge. It will keep for at least six months once opened.

SICILIAN FERMENTED EGGPLANT

This ferment has become an obsession on a par with kimchi. If it ends up taking up space in your fridge for the best part of a year, don't even consider throwing it out. The flavor really deepens with time, and you are sure to fall in love with it when the time is right. I never loved eggplants until I fermented them, and now we are inseparable. This will elevate a simple bowl of quinoa to something exotic. MAKES 1 X 1-QUART JAR

2 large eggplants, peeled and finely chopped

I to 2 garlic cloves, finely chopped

I bunch of fresh oregano, finely chopped

I teaspoon hot chili flakes

Sea salt (I tablespoon per 2¼ pounds of eggplant)

1 First weigh your eggplant, as you'll need one tablespoon of salt per 2¼ pounds of eggplants. After that, simply mix everything together in a bowl, then place into a clean 1-quart jar, making sure you leave 1 inch of headspace at the top of the jar.

2 Close the lid and leave in a warm place, ideally at 70°F, and check after seven days. This can ferment for up to four weeks, depending on the temperature and your desired flavor. When it's ready, store it in the fridge for up to six months.

FERMENTED BABA GHANOUSH

Baba ghanoush wins hands down over hummus for me. While a lot of the flavor in a traditional baba ghanoush is due to smoking the eggplants, this approach brings a new taste to the party. **MAKES 1 X 1-PINT JAR**

I eggplant, peeled and diced
....
I garlic clove, minced
....
I teaspoon smoked paprika
....
I teaspoon sea salt
....
4 tablespoons sesame seeds
....
Juice of 2 lemons
....
I tablespoon coconut milk
....
I tablespoon tahini
....
I teaspoon olive oil

1 Place the eggplant, garlic, paprika and salt in a bowl and leave for about five minutes, then massage the eggplant to release lots of juice. Press everything into a clean pint jar, making sure all the eggplant is covered in juice. Leave 1 inch of headspace at the top of the jar. Leave the jar in a warm spot for about two weeks.

2 To make the baba ghanoush, blitz the sesame seeds in a food processor until they are fine crumbs. Add the fermented eggplants, lemon juice, coconut milk , tahini, and olive oil and blitz until you get a thick, creamy puree. To elevate this to an elegant dip, garnish with a sprinkle of chopped fresh mint and parsley and a scattering of pomegranate seeds.

MUSHROOMS

I have a love–hate relationship with mushrooms. Sometime I love them, especially in a warming winter mushroom soup, while at other times the mere thought of them is disturbing. Maybe it's a seasonal thing. But the world of fungi is fascinating. Although it's a strange concept, we're actually more closely related to fungi than we are to any other kingdom.

The health benefits of mushrooms combined with the probiotic properties of fermentation give us a powerful homemade superfood. Just make sure the mushrooms you use are organically grown, because mushrooms absorb and concentrate whatever they grow in—good or bad.

I know this may seem like every shade of wrong, so perhaps it's one to bookmark for when your palate is more adventurous! For this fermentation mental shift, think antipasti and you will be a step closer to understanding the joy of this ferment. Fermented mushrooms can also be used in salads, raw sauces, or as the foundation of a wonderful probiotic mushroom pâté (see the recipe on the next page). However you use this ferment, it's worth trying someday. **MAKES 1 X 1-PINT JAR**

8 ounces button mushrooms, sliced or quartered
....
I onion, thinly sliced
....
I garlic clove, smashed
....
A few sprigs of fresh thyme
....
A few sprigs of fresh marjoram
....
4 percent brine solution (2 tablespoons sea salt per 4 cups of filtered water)

1 Place the mushrooms in a bowl with the sliced onion, garlic, and herbs, mixing them quickly to evenly integrate the ingredients. Pack a clean pint jar with the mushroom mix and top up with brine solution, making sure to leave 1 inch of headspace at the top of the jar and that the mushrooms are submerged in the brine.

2 Seal the jar and allow to ferment for five to seven days, then transfer to the fridge for longer storage. They will keep for many months, but I prefer to eat them within two to three weeks.

MUSHROOM PÂTÉ

Easily made, this classic dip takes a twist and can comfortably move beyond an appetizer to something more adventurous. It's a game changer added to a risotto at the last minute or dolloped on top of a pizza. Pair it happily with some mature fermented onions in a buckwheat crêpe. **MAKES 3 CUPS**

$^3/_4$ cup green lentils

I tablespoon coconut or olive oil, for sautéing

I small onion, diced

2 garlic cloves, minced

$^2/_3$ cup drained fermented mushrooms (page 86)

$^2/_3$ cup toasted walnuts or pecans

2 tablespoons minced fresh sage or flat-leaf parsley

2 tablespoons freshly squeezed lemon juice

I tablespoon tamari

2 teaspoons minced fresh rosemary

2 teaspoons minced fresh thyme

I teaspoon brown sugar

$^1/_8$ teaspoon cayenne pepper

Sea salt and freshly ground black pepper

1 Soak the lentils overnight. The next day, drain the lentils and place in a pot, then cover with fresh water. Bring to a boil, then reduce the heat to a simmer and cook for 40 minutes, until they have doubled in volume and are tender. Drain well. You will have about 2 cups of cooked lentils.

2 Heat the oil in a frying pan. Add the onion and garlic and cook, stirring frequently, for five to six minutes, until the onions are translucent.

3 Place the cooked lentils, drained fermented mushrooms, nuts, sage, lemon juice, tamari, rosemary, thyme, brown sugar, and cayenne pepper in a food processor. Scrape in the cooked onion and garlic and process until completely smooth. Taste and season with salt and pepper, adding additional tamari or lemon juice if it needs balancing.

4 Scrape the pâté into a small serving bowl and refrigerate for a few hours, until firm.

Leaves

The edible leaves of plants, such as bok choy, Brussels sprouts, cabbage, lettuce, radicchio, sorrel, spinach, Swiss chard, and watercress, make for excellent additions to ferments.

Delicate leaves don't lend themselves well to fermentation and are best mixed in with a more complex leaf, such as the more robust leaves of a cabbage.

INDIAN CHARD PICKLES

Leaves like chard will make a good kimchi and the chard stems make a delicious pickle. **MAKES 1 X 1-QUART JAR**

4 cups filtered water

1¹/₂ tablespoons sea salt

³/₄ tablespoon raw cane sugar

¹/₈ teaspoon ground turmeric

Pinch of ground cinnamon

I grape leaf (oak or horseradish will work too)

I teaspoon diced fresh ginger

2 cardamom pods

2 cloves

I small bay leaf

Pinch of coriander seeds

3 to 4 bunches of Swiss chard

1 Bring the water to a boil and stir in the salt, sugar, turmeric, and cinnamon until dissolved.

2 Place the grape leaf at the bottom of a clean 1-quart jar (this helps the pickle to stay crunchy), then add the ginger and spices to the jar. Pack the jar tightly with the upright Swiss chard stems, then pour the warm brine over the stems to the very top of the jar, ensuring that each one is below the surface of the brine.

3 Cover and place in a dark corner to ferment for three days at room temperature, then store in the fridge for up to two months.

WILD GARLIC LEAVES

Reserved as my little ritual to celebrate the start of spring and the promise of new growth to gather, I like to carefully forage some wild garlic from the few abundant patches I know. I pick enough to make pesto and some extra to ferment as whole leaves to be used as a garnish. These can also be used as a wrap for all kinds of fillings. **MAKES 1 X 1-QUART JAR**

2¹/₄ pounds wild garlic, washed well

I tablespoon sea salt (if using the dry salting method)

2 percent brine solution (I tablespoon sea salt dissolved in 4 cups filtered water) (if using the salinity method)

1 You can use one of two methods to ferment your wild garlic leaves. You can place the leaves in a bowl and massage them with one tablespoon of salt to create enough liquid, then place this wet mixture into a clean 1-quart jar, packing it tightly and submerging the leaves in their own juices. Or you can pack the leaves into a jar as tightly as possible, then pour in enough 2 percent brine solution to cover them and submerge them with a weight. Either way, leave 1 inch of headspace at the top of the jar.

2 Seal the jar and leave for one week to ferment at room temperature, then store in the fridge for up to two months.

Ways to use leftover brine

Even when you've munched your way through a jar of homemade pickles, don't throw out that brine! Before you consider committing such a heinous crime as pouring brine down the sink, consider this: that brine is teeming with beneficial bacteria and gut-healing goodness. Reusing your brine is home economics at its finest, sure to make your mother proud.

- Use it as a salad dressing to add a little tang—just mix it with oil.

- Drink it straight. Have you ever heard of the old-fashioned remedy of drinking pickle juice to cure a hangover? Or even a pickleback?

- Add it to your Bloody Mary.

- Add a splash to your fresh juice or smoothie.

- Reuse it as an optional starter for other ferments (four tablespoons per quart).

- Use it as a marinade for meat or fish (you can also use kombucha and kefir to marinate meat).

- Mix into rice and stir-fries.

- Add it to cooled soup, as on page 192.

- Use it to make your condiments, like the mayo on page 115.

FRUIT

FRUIT FERMENTS ARE very similar to vegetables. Fermenting fruit involves placing your chosen fruit in a jar or other container and adding a combination of water, sugar, and starter culture. The lid is then sealed and the fruit is left at room temperature for two to ten days. Leave them too long, though, and you'll end up with a tangy alcoholic compote to top your breakfast with!

The main difference between fruit and vegetable ferments is the intentional addition of a starter to fruit, which helps keep the ferment from turning alcoholic. The starter adds the bacteria that will help the good lactic acid bacteria take off before the alcohol-producing yeast do. Go for ripe, organic produce with no bruises or blemishes, as these spoilages may affect your ferment by introducing unfavorable bacteria.

The most common starter cultures for fermenting fruit are whey or baking yeast. You can also use an opened probiotic capsule, the liquid from a previously opened jar of fermented fruit, or a fermented beverage such as plain kombucha tea (page 302), water kefir (page 280), or a ginger bug (page 284–285). Carbon dioxide gas will be produced as a by-product, so watch out for those bubbles at the top of the jar.

A wide variety of fruit is suitable for fermenting:
- Fruits like **peaches**, **plums**, and **apricots** are a popular choice for fermenting, as they are tasty and hold their color well. Wash the fruit, peel the skin if they aren't organic, and remove any pits.
- **Exotic fruits** like mangoes and pineapples ferment well too and can be used to make chutney. Remove the skins and cut into even-sized cubes before using. However, be mindful that these fruits contain a lot of sugar, so they ferment with vigor!
- **Grapes** can be fermented, but they must be pricked with a needle or cut in half to allow the cultured liquid to get inside. Otherwise you'll have balls of wine to get your taste buds and your head around!

- **Peeled and sliced pears** can be fermented, as can apples, but be warned that apples tend to turn brown in the process. This doesn't bother me, but some people find it unappealing.
- Most **berries** can be fermented, except for blackberries, which contain too many seeds. You can combat this, though, if you pass them through a fine-mesh sieve to remove the seeds. Strawberries are a little difficult to ferment, as they are quite acidic. They're best enjoyed in season with cream! Having said that, though, they can be used to flavor a huge range of fermented drinks (see page 295).

Once fermented, the fruit will contain an abundance of beneficial bacteria and can be used as a condiment, dessert topping, or in recipes for things like chutneys, smoothies, and salsas.

Fruit tends to ferment quickly, in 24 to 48 hours. The length of time you allow your fruit to ferment is a matter of personal preference. Tasting often is advisable so that you can find the perfect length of time for you. For further experimentation, you can replace the fruit as you go—this will keep the fermentation process going indefinitely.

Fermented fruits should have a pleasantly sour taste and should hold their original shape. They should not taste rotten. Use your logic and innate judgment.

LACTO-FERMENTED BLUEBERRIES

Blueberries, hailed as a superfood for their antioxidant properties, are pleasant but not overly distinctive in taste. They're sweet and fresh with a hint of tart, but there's room for a little fermented flavor manipulation. In this fruit ferment, live cultures from the brine, whey, or other source is used purely to allow the bacteria to go straight to work on the sugar—allowing us to lower the amount of salt and avoid a strange sweet-and-salty taste. However, if you prefer, you can just use the regular 2 percent brine. **MAKES 1 X 1-PINT JAR**

1 pound blueberries

2 tablespoons maple syrup, raw honey, or raw cane sugar

2 tablespoons whey or water kefir (page 280)

$1/4$ teaspoon sea salt

Filtered water

1 Place the berries, maple syrup, whey or water kefir, and sea salt in a bowl and mix together. Pack the berry mixture into a clean pint jar. Lightly press down on the berries to help them fit in the jar. Add enough water to cover the berries completely, but make sure you leave 1 inch of headspace at the top of the jar. Place your favorite fermentation weight on top of the berries to keep them submerged (see pages 21—23 for ideas).

2 Pop the lid on and leave to ferment at room temperature for 24 hours, then refrigerate and use within two to three weeks.

LACTO-FERMENTED GRAPES

I know you're thinking wine, but I'm promoting these as probiotics! Enjoy these as a sweet and salty addition to any of your salads or cheeseboards. In this fruit ferment, live cultures from the brine, whey, or other source is used purely to allow the bacteria to go straight to work on the sugar—allowing us to lower the amount of salt and avoid a strange sweet-and-salty taste. However, if you prefer, you can just use the regular 2 percent brine. **MAKES 1 X 1-PINT JAR**

1 pound grapes

2 tablespoons whey or water kefir (page 280)

$1/4$ teaspoon sea salt

Filtered water

Give these a try by popping them in a jar as you would with the blueberries in the previous recipe. Just pierce the skin first with a sterilized needle and there's no need for the maple syrup.

BANANAS

I can sense your reluctance to bend your brain around this ferment, but this could be your best ferment yet! It's tart, fizzy, and slightly sweet, and the smell is really banana-y. Best of all, the sugar-loving bacteria have taken care of the fructose overload the banana delivers when eaten raw. In this fruit ferment, live cultures from the brine, whey, or other source is used purely to allow the bacteria to go straight to work on the sugar—allowing us to lower the amount of salt and avoid a strange sweet-and-salty taste. However, if you prefer, you can just use the regular 2 percent brine. **MAKES 1 X 1-PINT JAR**

Filtered water

2 bananas, cut into medium slices

4 to 6 tablespoons whey or water kefir (page 280)

2 tablespoons raw brown cane sugar

Sea salt

1 Half-fill a clean pint jar with filtered water. For each banana that you use, add two to three tablespoons of whey or water kefir (or you could use the contents of a probiotic capsule), one tablespoon of raw brown cane sugar, and a generous pinch of sea salt. Add the chopped bananas, leaving 1 inch headspace at the top of the jar. Submerge the contents with a weight.

2 Close the jar and let it sit out for two to three days at room temperature. Bananas will ferment much faster with this added starter, so check them after two days, as they can start to get fairly alcoholic and lose almost all their sweetness. They will keep in the fridge for two weeks. Enjoy with some ice cream or caramel sauce.

PRESERVED LEMONS

You cannot be without these juicy, radiant jewels in a jar. Preserved lemons will transform your culinary creations from good to sensational, and they are so easy and quick to make. They are used throughout Morocco, the Middle East, and in certain areas of India to bring a special twist to dishes. Use them to flavor a grain-based salad, stir them through sauces, add them to seafood, poultry, and roasted vegetables, mix a little into your hummus and pesto . . . the possibilities are endless. **MAKES 1 X 1-QUART JAR**

8 organic unwaxed lemons

1/3 cup unrefined sea salt

OPTIONAL ADD-INS:

I fresh chili

I bay leaf

I cinnamon stick

I sprig of fresh thyme

Cardamom seeds

1 Clean the lemons well. Organic is best, with unwaxed coming in second place, since it's the lemon rinds you'll be eating. Trim the ends off the lemons, taking care not to cut into the flesh, then slice the lemons three-quarters of the way down, as if to quarter them, but keeping the base of the lemon intact. Place the lemons in a big bowl and sprinkle the insides of each one with one tablespoon of the unrefined sea salt. Let them sit for 30 minutes to allow the salt to draw out the lemon juice.

2 After this time, start to layer the lemons and the remaining salt in your clean 1-quart jar. Press each lemon in with a pounder or wooden spoon. The lemons will release their juice, which will combine with the salt to create a brine conducive to the proliferation of beneficial bacteria. Continue adding and mashing, adding any optional extras too, until the jar is filled. Top up with any residual lemon juice and salt from the bowl so that the lemons are all completely covered with the brine. Use a weight to keep them submerged, making sure you leave 1 inch of headspace at the top of the jar.

3 Ferment at room temperature for three to four weeks. Lemons can be kept for one to two years at room temperature, but I have never had them long enough to really know—I get through them in no time at all.

Lacto-fermented relishes and chutneys

I often use the terms *relish* and *chutney* with interchangeable ease, but to define their differences simply, relishes have a bit of chunk, whereas chutneys have a smooth, uniform texture. Like all good preserves, they make the best of the harvest, but my selection seems to heavily favor their position on the Indian plate. It might come as no surprise that the word *chutney* is a translation of *chatni*, meaning "side dish."

LIME PICKLE

You know things have gotten serious when you start making your own fermented relish for your curry night. So instead of picking up a store-bought Indian chutney, look for some asafetida in your local Asian shop instead. This pungent Indian cooking essential mellows out to give a pleasant onion and garlic taste.
MAKES 1 X ½-GALLON JAR

18 organic limes

4 tablespoons sea salt

3 tablespoons ground turmeric

1 tablespoon white wine vinegar

1 cup olive oil

7 tablespoons mustard seeds

8 teaspoons fenugreek seeds, crushed

3 tablespoons cayenne pepper

1 tablespoon asafetida powder

1 Cut each lime into eight segments. Place the cut limes in a small fermenting crock or a clean ½-gallon jar and toss with the salt, turmeric, and vinegar. Pack this mixture down and place a weight over the top, making sure you leave 1 inch of headspace at the top of the jar. Cover loosely with a lid, allowing gas pressure to escape. If you're using a tightly sealed jar, remember to burp it every so often.

2 Leave to ferment for four weeks. After this time the lime peel will be soft and edible. At this stage add the olive oil, mustard seeds, crushed fenugreek seeds, cayenne pepper, and asafetida—mix, shake, or massage it all in with the softened limes. Leave in a closed jar for another one to two weeks to give the flavors a chance to infuse. When you're happy with the taste, store in the fridge for up to six months.

APPLE RELISH

When autumn gives you apples, there is sometimes no choice but to make something of it. Apples will easily pair with a multitude of flavors, but this recipe takes a fresh, zesty, herbal, sweet, warming approach. Adding a starter will make this a quick ferment. Fruit ferments do not usually last very long, so enjoy while it is young. **MAKES 1 X 1-PINT JAR**

I pound apples (any kind), chopped

I teaspoon sea salt

$^1/_2$ teaspoon water kefir (page 280), ginger bug (pages 284–285), or fresh whey

OPTIONAL EXTRAS:

Zest of $^1/_2$ orange

Zest of $^1/_2$ lemon

A few fresh mint leaves

A few sprigs of fresh rosemary

I vanilla bean, split in half lengthways and seeds scraped out

I cinnamon stick

I teaspoon whole cloves

1 Place the apples, salt, and starter in a food processor and pulse, but leave it quite coarse.

2 Transfer to a bowl and stir in your chosen extras, if using, then transfer to a clean pint jar, making sure the contents are submerged in liquid and that you leave 1 inch of headspace at the top of the jar.

3 Leave to ferment for three days at room temperature. Taste after this time, and if you're happy with the flavor, store it in the fridge and eat within two to three weeks.

APPLE FIVE-SPICE RELISH

You can easily substitute pears for the apples for a pear five-spice relish instead. **MAKES 1 X 1-QUART JAR**

I$^1/_2$ pounds apples (any kind), coarsely chopped

$^1/_2$ cup lemon juice

4 tablespoons whey, water kefir (page 280), kombucha (page 302), or ginger bug (pages 284–285)

I teaspoon sea salt

I cup raisins

I cup pecans or other nut, chopped

4 tablespoons coconut sugar, date paste, or other natural sweetener

4 teaspoons Chinese five-spice blend

I cup filtered water (optional)

1 Place the apples, lemon juice, starter, and salt in a food processor and pulse, leaving it quite coarse. Transfer to a bowl and add the raisins, chopped nuts, sugar, and five-spice blend. Mix it together well, then pack into a clean 1-quart jar, making sure all the ingredients are covered in liquid. Top up with the filtered water if necessary, making sure you leave 1 inch of headspace at the top of the jar.

2 Leave to ferment for two to three days at room temperature, then transfer to the fridge and enjoy within two to three weeks.

INDIAN RELISH

If you're making the lime pickle on page 98, then you might as well make this too for a plate that truly sings. Variety is the spice of life.

MAKES 1 X ¹/₂-GALLON JAR

6 organic unwaxed lemons

¹/₂ cup sea salt

¹/₂ cup raw cane sugar

2 to 4 tablespoons chili powder (depending on how hot you like it)

3 teaspoons ground turmeric

I teaspoon fenugreek seeds

I teaspoon black mustard seeds

¹/₄ teaspoon asafetida powder

Juice of I lemon

1 Chop the lemons into small chunks and place in a clean ¹/₂-gallon jar with the salt, sugar, chili powder, and turmeric.

2 Toast the fenugreek and mustard seeds in a hot, dry pan set over a medium heat just until they are aromatic. Allow to cool slightly, then grind the seeds into a powder and mix in the asafetida. Add to the jar along with the lemon juice. Place a weight on top of the mixture, making sure all the lemon chunks are submerged and you have left 1 inch of headspace at the top of the jar.

3 Leave to ferment for two months somewhere warm, preferably in a sunny spot in the kitchen. This can be transferred to the fridge when fermented for long-term storage for up to a year.

PINEAPPLE AND MINT RELISH

I love how fermentation has enlightened me to make many things from one purchase. Not only can I make my pineapple relish, but I can also make the most delicious fermented drink, tepache, from the leftover pineapple skin (see the recipe on page 291). This is radical home economics!

MAKES 1 X 1-QUART JAR

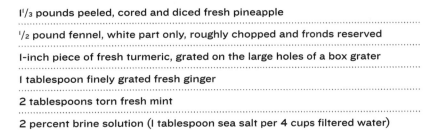

1¹/₃ pounds peeled, cored and diced fresh pineapple

¹/₂ pound fennel, white part only, roughly chopped and fronds reserved

1-inch piece of fresh turmeric, grated on the large holes of a box grater

1 tablespoon finely grated fresh ginger

2 tablespoons torn fresh mint

2 percent brine solution (1 tablespoon sea salt per 4 cups filtered water)

1 Mix the pineapple, fennel, fennel fronds, turmeric, ginger, and mint in a bowl. Place in a clean 1-quart jar, then cover with the brine. Cover with a weight to keep it from floating to the top and make sure to leave 1 inch of headspace at the top of the jar.

2 Leave the jar on the counter for three days. If you're using sealed jars, such as Le Parfait or Fido jars, which have a tight seal with no chance for the air to escape, then remember to burp the jar every day. Pineapple contains lots of sugar so it will ferment fast, creating a lot of carbon dioxide, and you want to avoid an explosion! Transfer to the fridge after three days and eat within two weeks. Due to the high sugar content of the pineapple, it can become quite acidic very quickly.

RHUBARB SALSA

Life is too short to only make rhubarb crumble. Plus, when that sugar buzz leaves your palate, what else is there to do other than ferment it? This is a pretty neat little twist that might leave gardeners scratching their heads with consideration. **MAKES 1 X 1-QUART JAR**

7 to 8 rhubarb stalks, coarsely chopped

¹/₂ green pepper, deseeded and diced

¹/₂ small red onion, finely diced

1 to 2 jalapeño peppers, deseeded and finely chopped

2- to 3-inch piece of fresh ginger, peeled and finely grated

¹/₂ cup raw honey

Juice of 1 lemon

Zest of 1 orange

1 teaspoon sea salt (or 2 percent of the total weight of ingredients)

1 Soften the rhubarb by simmering it in a few tablespoons of filtered water in a pan set over a medium heat for ten to 15 minutes. Remove the rhubarb from the heat when it begins to fall apart and place it in a blender or food processor. Add all the remaining ingredients—including the whey or sauerkraut brine if you want it to ferment—and blend together until a chunky puree is formed. (If you're working by hand, just mix everything together well in a large bowl.) Spoon into a clean 1-quart jar, leaving 1 inch of headspace at the top of the jar.

2 Let it sit at room temperature for one to two days, then store in the refrigerator for three to four weeks.

RAISIN AND SPICE RELISH

This will perk up anything from a simple meal to a rich curry. As a flavorful condiment, it's pretty perfect. **MAKES 1 X 1-PINT JAR**

1¼ cups raisins

1 small bunch of cilantro, leaves finely chopped

2 garlic cloves, crushed

10 black peppercorns

1 tablespoon coriander seeds

½ tablespoon cumin seeds

½ tablespoon freshly grated ginger

¼ teaspoon chili flakes

1 teaspoon sea salt (or 2 percent of the total weight of ingredients)

½ cup filtered water (optional)

1 First place the raisins in a small bowl. Cover with filtered water and let them soak for one hour.

2 Pulse the cilantro and garlic together in a food processor. Drain the raisins and add them to the food processer along with the peppercorns, coriander seeds, cumin seeds, ginger, and chili flakes. Pulse a few times until the mixture is a chunky paste.

3 Scoop the paste into a clean pint jar, pressing the relish down to raise the juices. Mix the salt into the whey or water kefir to make a brine, then pour it into the jar, leaving 1 inch of headspace at the top of the jar. Top up with filtered water to fill the jar to this level if needed. Use your weight of choice to help submerge the contents and cover the jar with a lid.

4 Leave to ferment for two to three days, then transfer to the fridge and enjoy within two to three weeks, after which time the relish will develop a distinctly boozy taste.

COCONUT CHUTNEY

It's evident I love Indian spice. I also love kefir (see page 133 for more on that), so this is a beautiful union of my two favorite things to give me something truly tasty that's bursting with flavor, enzymes, vitamins, and fermented goodness.

MAKES 1 X 1-PINT JAR

2 cups shredded, unsweetened, unsulfured coconut

1/2 cup warm filtered water

1/2 cup milk kefir (page 134) or coconut milk kefir (page 144)

Juice of 1 lemon

1 tablespoon raw honey

1 teaspoon cumin seeds

1 teaspoon coriander seeds

1 teaspoon sea salt

1/2 teaspoon mustard seeds

1 Put the coconut in a small bowl and pour the water over it. Allow to soak for five minutes.

2 Whiz all the ingredients in a blender until well combined. Transfer to a clean pint jar, making sure you leave 1 inch of headspace at the top of the jar.

3 Leave at room temperature for two to four days, or until you see pockets of air indicating micro-organism action. Transfer to the fridge after this time and eat within two months.

MANGO CHUTNEY

Whether you eat meat, fish, veggies, or vegan, this condiment will enliven your plate. It's sweet, spicy, warm, and tangy. Mix with some fresh avocado as a great little accompanimemt.

MAKES 1 X 1-PINT JAR

2 ripe mangoes, peeled and diced

1 apple, peeled, cored and diced

1 red pepper, deseeded and diced

3 tablespoons minced fresh ginger

1 tablespoon minced garlic

1 teaspoon minced chili pepper

Sea salt (2 tablespoons per 1 pound of fruit)

1 Mix everything together in a bowl and place in a clean pint fermentation jar. Leave 1 inch of headspace at the top of the jar, then tightly screw on a lid with a fermentation lock. Add water in the lock.

2 Leave in a warm place (approximately 75°F) and check after two days. Transfer to the fridge, where it will keep for up to one month.

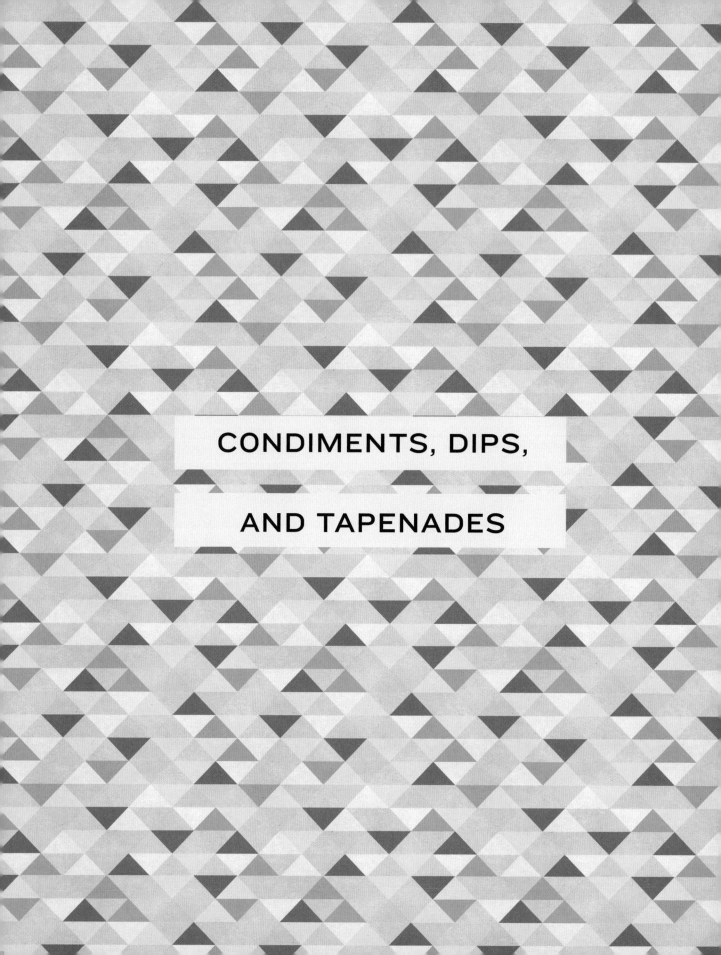

CONDIMENTS, DIPS,

AND TAPENADES

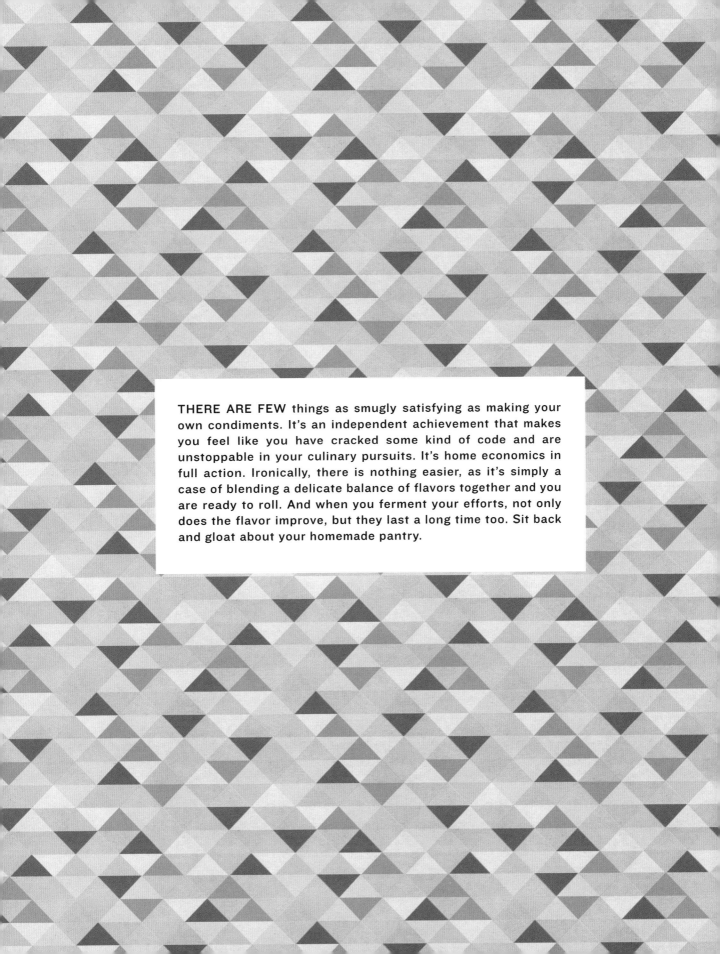

THERE ARE FEW things as smugly satisfying as making your own condiments. It's an independent achievement that makes you feel like you have cracked some kind of code and are unstoppable in your culinary pursuits. It's home economics in full action. Ironically, there is nothing easier, as it's simply a case of blending a delicate balance of flavors together and you are ready to roll. And when you ferment your efforts, not only does the flavor improve, but they last a long time too. Sit back and gloat about your homemade pantry.

DUKKAH

Life before dukkah seems bland in comparison. Dukkah is an Egyptian condiment, and this lush recipe is from Maggie Lynch, director of cooking studies at the Irish Institute of Nutrition. Your house will smell amazing and you will not regret making a stash of it.

MAKES 1 X 12-OUNCE JAR

3/4 cup skinned hazelnuts or whole almonds or pistachio nuts, with their skins

4 tablespoons sesame seeds

3 tablespoons cumin seeds

I 1/2 tablespoons coriander seeds

I teaspoon fennel seeds

2 tablespoons sunflower seeds

I tablespoon pink peppercorns

I teaspoon nigella seeds

2 teaspoons ground nori

2 teaspoons chia seeds

I 1/2 teaspoons sea salt

I teaspoon smoked paprika

I teaspoon ground cinnamon

1 Toast the nuts in a dry pan set over a medium heat for a few minutes. Shake the pan constantly to prevent them from burning. Transfer to a food processor and pulse to a fine or coarse crumble, then tip into a bowl. Alternatively, using a mortar and pestle for crushing the nuts will give you more control of the texture.

2 Using the same hot, dry pan, toast the sesame seeds as above and add to the bowl with the nuts, then lightly toast the cumin, coriander, and fennel seeds. Transfer them immediately to the food processor.

3 Dry toast the sunflower seeds, as above, followed by the pink peppercorns and nigella seeds. Transfer to the food processor or your mortar and pestle. Pulse or crush all the seeds together, but don't over-process. Finally, add in the ground nori, chia seeds, sea salt, smoked paprika, and cinnamon to the nut bowl, then mix together with the coarsely chopped seeds. Store in an airtight container, at the ready to sprinkle on everything.

FURIKAKE

This Japanese seasoning will henceforth transform your rice dishes, but its joys don't have to stop there—you can use it to season many other dishes. **MAKES 1 X 1-PINT JAR**

1/2 cup raw sesame seeds

1 teaspoon to 1 tablespoon sea salt

3 sheets of nori

3 heaped tablespoons bonito flakes (optional)

3 tablespoons milled wakame

1/2 teaspoon wasabi powder (optional)

1/2 teaspoon raw cane sugar (optional)

1 Heat a dry pan over a medium-high heat. Pour in the sesame seeds and shake to distribute them evenly over the surface of the pan. Toast, shaking occasionally, until the seeds are fragrant and begin making little popping sounds. Immediately pour the seeds into a dry, clean bowl to cool, then stir in the sea salt to taste. Allow to cool completely before proceeding.

2 Use kitchen shears or clean, dry scissors to cut the nori into 1-inch-wide strips. Stack the strips and cut them crosswise into very thin strips over the bowl of sesame seeds. Use the kitchen shears again to roughly cut up the bonito flakes, if using. Add the wakame, wasabi powder, and sugar, if using. Stir all the ingredients together, then transfer to a jar with a tight-fitting lid.

3 This is ready to use immediately but can be stored in a cool, dry place out of direct sunlight for up to two months.

YANGNYEOMJANG DIPPING SAUCE

An indispensable condiment that will liven up anything from tofu to fresh vegetables. It comes to the rescue if cooking something complicated is out of the question. Pair it with a kimchi pancake (page 226) and you will never look back. **MAKES 1/4 CUP**

1 spring onion, chopped

1 fermented garlic clove (page 68), grated

3 tablespoons tamari

1 tablespoon sesame oil

2 teaspoons Korean red pepper powder (gochugaru)

2 teaspoons black or white sesame seeds, toasted

1/2 teaspoon raw honey

1/2 teaspoon kombucha vinegar (page 318)

Combine all the ingredients in a small bowl. It will keep well for three days in the fridge.

Lacto-fermented mustards

You will be beyond thrilled when you realize how simple it is to make your own mustard, especially if you have half jars of old brine sitting around awaiting a new adventure. I didn't care much for mustard before I started making my own, but now it finds its way into regular use.

KOMBUCHA MUSTARD

I have an unblended bottle of kombucha and mustard seeds in my cupboard that has been there for more than a year. I must have forgotten to blend it, but every so often I will use a drop for an intense hit of something tart and spicy. On a culinary whim, I have used a splash of this when recipes call for both vinegar and mustard. But before you find yourself in the same boat, here is what you can do.

MAKES 1 X ½-PINT JAR

6 tablespoons brown or yellow mustard seeds (brown are hotter and will make a spicier mustard)

³/₄ cup overbrewed kombucha (page 302)

1 tablespoon raw apple cider vinegar (more or less according to your preferred tang)

1 teaspoon ground turmeric

Pinch of sea salt

1 Place the mustard seeds in a clean pint jar. Pour in the kombucha, making sure it covers the seeds. Leave 1 inch of headspace at the top of the jar.

2 Screw on the lid and let it sit on the counter for two to three weeks, burping the jar every few days. After this time, place in a blender with the vinegar, turmeric, and salt. Process until well blended and top up with water or more kombucha until it's your desired consistency. Transfer to a clean ½-pint jar and leave out at room temperature to ferment for another three days, then transfer to the fridge, where it will keep for six months—or for over a year in my case!

QUICK MUSTARD TO USE UP YOUR BRINE

Similar to the recipe for kombucha mustard on the previous page, this is a quick mustard to use up your leftover brine. **MAKES 1 X ½-PINT JAR**

²/₃ cup brown or yellow mustard seeds (or both)

³/₄ cup pickle brine

¹/₂ tablespoon minced garlic

I tablespoon raw honey or maple syrup

1 Combine the mustard seeds, pickle brine, and garlic in a bowl and allow to soak at room temperature overnight.

2 The next day, tip the soaked seeds into a blender with the honey and blend to your desired texture.

3 Transfer to a clean ½-pint jar and let it sit on the counter for two to three days. Taste and check the seasoning, adjusting if necessary. Store in a sealed jar in the fridge, where it will keep for many months.

Lacto-fermented sauces and dips

There are many satisfying things about fermenting, one of which being the fact that your culinary efforts are preserved. It's annoying to make a fresh mayonnaise or hummus and hear the shelf life clock ticking— personally, I don't want to eat the same thing three days in a row. It's easy to see how processed convenience food was welcomed. When you ferment these delights, though, you are giving a natural preservation powerhouse to these foods and giving yourself a little more time to enjoy the fancier things in life.

LACTO-FERMENTED MAYONNAISE

Mayonnaise never really featured on my shopping list. I'm not sure why—perhaps it was due to a deep mistrust of how white is was. Curiosity led me to make a homemade fermented mayonnaise, and to my delight, my children loved it. There's nothing like a child's approval to encourage further culinary creations. Homemade fermented mayonnaise will change your world and many dishes. For me, sweet potatoes, pumpkins, and butternut squash seem naked without it slathered on.

There are many wonderful variations of this mayonnaise, so work with whatever you have in your fermenting fridge.

- *The kombucha vinegar can be substituted with apple cider, rice, or champagne vinegar, or **get creative** with your favorite flavored vinegar.*
- *Brine juice can be **substituted** with whey or lemon juice.*
- *The salt can be **substituted** with one tablespoon of miso.*
- *You can **funk this up** with wasabi, garlic powder, herbs, or lemon zest.*
- *For a **vegan version** of this mayonnaise, you can easily substitute each egg yolk with three tablespoons of aquafaba (the reserved liquid from a can of chickpeas).*
- *Add a pinch of turmeric and black pepper for **color** and **extra nutrition**.*

MAKES 1 X ½-PINT JAR

2 egg yolks

I tablespoon homemade fermented mustard (page II2) or ¼ teaspoon mustard powder

I tablespoon kombucha vinegar (page 3I8)

I tablespoon brine juice

¼ teaspoon sea salt or to taste

I cup avocado, grapeseed, or mild olive oil (my preference is grapeseed oil)

All ingredients should be at room temperature before you start.

1 Place the egg yolks, mustard, vinegar, brine juice, and salt in a food processor. Blend for about 30 seconds, until well combined.

2 With the food processor running, add the oil in as slow a drizzle as possible to emulsify into mayonnaise. It takes me at least three minutes to slowly pour in the oil drip by drip and complete the emulsification. Adjust the salt to taste.

3 Transfer to a clean ½-pint jar and leave out at room temperature for two to three days, then transfer to the fridge, where it will keep for at least one month.

Don't throw out your eggshells!

Eggshells are a fantastic source of absorbable calcium and have many great uses around your home. They're a great addition to fertilizer, they're fantastic for making coffee taste less bitter, they're good for garden pest control, and wonderful for your pet food or chicken feed. And if your pets can eat it, then why can't you?

High-quality eggshells contain 27 essential microelements, but they're mostly composed of calcium carbonate in a form and structure that's similar to our bones and teeth. If you grind eggshells into a very fine powder, it's a wonderful source of calcium that can be added to a variety of meals, smoothies, or porridge oats.

To make the powder, collect about 20 organic, free-range eggshells. There's no need to remove the membrane, as it has extra nutrients. Boil them in water for about five minutes to kill any bacteria, making sure the shells are fully submerged. Once they're clean and dried, pop them into a good blender (a NutriBullet does a fine job) and whiz into a powder.

If the idea of hiding some calcium in your food doesn't appeal, then pop them into a capsule as a homemade supplement. However, the recommended dosage is no more than one teaspoon a day, as it can irritate sensitive digestive tracts.

LACTO-FERMENTED KETCHUP

Even the simplest meal can be transformed into a dish of culinary excellence with a bit of this ketchup. If you've never tasted fermented tomato sauce and fermented potatoes (see page 65), then get ready for your taste buds to never look back. I do feel rather smug when my kids indulge in this ketchup. It's a small victory on the continuous parental cooking challenge. This ketchup also works well on savory pancakes.

MAKES 1 X 1-PINT JAR

I cup tomato puree

3 small garlic cloves, minced

$^1/_3$ cup raw honey or maple syrup

6 tablespoons sauerkraut juice or whey

3 tablespoons raw apple cider vinegar

$2^1/_4$ teaspoons fine sea salt

Pinch of cayenne pepper

1 Place all the ingredients in a blender and blend to combine. Transfer to a clean pint jar, making sure you leave 1 inch of headspace at the top of the jar.

2 Seal the lid and allow to ferment for two to five days, then store in the fridge, where it will keep for two months.

KOMBUCHA KETCHUP WITH A LITTLE SPICE

Because variety is the spice of life, I love a good variation on a theme. Both of the ketchup recipes have their merits, so it's always good to mix and match. ***MAKES 1 X 1-PINT JAR***

I$^2/_3$ cups tomato puree

$^1/_3$ to $^1/_2$ cup coconut sugar or rapadura, or 3 tablespoons maple syrup

$^2/_3$ to I cup kombucha vinegar (page 318)

$^1/_8$ teaspoon ground cinnamon

$^1/_8$ teaspoon ground cloves

$^1/_8$ teaspoon cayenne pepper

$^1/_8$ teaspoon ground black pepper

Sea salt, to taste

Follow the same method as for the lacto-fermented ketchup.

HAPPY FERMENTED CHILI SAUCE

There are those who cannot live without their chili fix. For some it's the ultimate feel-good food, as the body releases endorphins to deal with the heat. I have modified my cooking somewhat since having kids, so the notion of anything spicy has been relegated to the status of "occasional condiment," as it seems there are already enough endorphin-inducing moments in my day. Catering to all palates is easily fixed by having a bottle or jar of chili sauce on hand, ready to use as necessary.

If you're wondering what type of chili to use for your recipe, you can test a chili by rubbing a small piece of the flesh against your lip or nibbling a tiny piece off the end. This will give you enough of an indication of where it registers on the heat scale. MAKES 1 X ½-PINT JAR

12 chili peppers
....
6 garlic cloves
....
2-inch piece of fresh ginger, peeled
....
2-inch piece of fresh turmeric, peeled
....
2 tablespoons lime juice
....
1 teaspoon sea salt
....
Pinch of freshly ground black pepper

1 Place the whole peppers and garlic cloves, ginger, turmeric, lime juice, and salt and pepper in a food processor. Blend until everything is chopped up quite fine and is nearly a liquidy paste. Place in a clean ½-pint jar, making sure you leave 1 inch of headspace at the top of the jar.

2 Leave it out on the countertop for two to five weeks, stirring occasionally and tasting as you go before unleashing the chili buzz. This will keep in the fridge for at least six months.

LEMONY HUMMUS

I remember being thrilled with my first batch of hummus many years ago. Looking back, it was more like cement, but student kitchens were never well equipped and student palates are a little easier to impress. I would get creative with some funky dips but was always hugely frustrated that my efforts would either need to be eaten for the next three days straight or it would be making its way to the trash. One thing that always keeps me giddy about fermentation is the fact that all your efforts are preserved. A batch of freshly made hummus will stay good for at least two weeks in the fridge. **MAKES 1 X 1-PINT JAR**

2 cups (I x 16-ounce can) chickpeas, drained and rinsed

2 garlic cloves, grated

$1/4$ cup freshly squeezed lemon juice or $1/2$ preserved lemon (page 97)

2 tablespoons whey or brine juice

$1/2$ teaspoon ground cumin

$1/2$ teaspoon smoked paprika

$1/3$ cup flax or avocado oil

$1/2$ cup tahini

I teaspoon sea salt

Freshly ground black pepper

1 Place the chickpeas, garlic, lemon juice, whey, and spices in a food processor or blender and pulse until smooth. Add the oil, tahini, sea salt, and a little black pepper, then blend again until well mixed. Transfer to a clean pint jar, making sure you leave 1 inch of headspace at the top of the jar.

2 Leave on the counter to ferment for two days, then store in the fridge for up to two weeks.

Olives

Olives are too bitter to eat straight from the tree and are made edible and savory by various processes, including soaking them in oil, brine, or water or dry packing them in salt. Sadly, commercial olives are soaked in a harsh chemical called lye, which removes the bitterness but also a lot of the flavor. When choosing olives for their health benefits and their flavor, always choose ones that have been traditionally cured. The stronger-flavored, traditional Greek olives found in olive bars or the refrigerated section of health food stores are not treated with lye and are still alive with active cultures. They're also a great source of iron, vitamin E, and dietary fiber.

GREEN OLIVE AND PRESERVED LEMON TAPENADE

I like to tart up any dish with a little burst of flavor, and this zingy tapenade will do just that.
MAKES 1 X ½-PINT JAR

I whole preserved lemon (page 97) or ½ cup fresh lemon juice

I cup pitted green olives

5 garlic cloves, peeled

¼ cup olive oil

1 If you prefer, preserved lemons can be rinsed before they're eaten to remove some of the excess salt from the fermentation process, so just give them a quick once-over under cold running water, then toss it in your food processor or blender. Add the green olives, garlic, and olive oil and pulse a few times. Pulsing is better for tapenade because you don't want to blend everything into a uniform paste. You want things to mix well but remain a bit chunky.

2 Spoon into a clean ½-pint jar or airtight container and pour a little olive oil over the top to protect the top from oxidation. Store in the fridge for up to two months.

FIG AND OLIVE TAPENADE

Sweet, savory, floral and ready to transform an impromptu plate. **MAKES 1 X 1-PINT JAR**

¾ cup dried figs, roughly chopped

⅔ cup Kalamata olives, pitted

⅔ cup green olives, pitted

3 tablespoons extra virgin olive oil, plus extra for the top

I tablespoon kombucha vinegar (page 318)

I teaspoon minced fresh rosemary

Place all the ingredients in a food processor and pulse a few times. Spoon into a clean pint jar or airtight container and pour a little olive oil over the top to protect the top from oxidation. Store in the fridge for up to two months.

BEET TAPENADE

While this is not technically a ferment, I love a little variation on a theme. This beet tapenade works wonderfully well with something spicy, on the side of a cheeseboard or spread over a savory pancake. You could use the beet left over from beet kvass (page 297) in this recipe. **MAKES 1 X 1-PINT JAR**

¹/₄ cup extra virgin olive oil

I tablespoon minced onion

I tablespoon minced garlic

I pound fermented beets from kvass (page 297), chopped

²/₃ cup pitted black Kalamata olives

I organic and unwaxed lemon, zest of ¹/₂ and juice of the whole lemon

I tablespoon finely chopped fresh herbs (parsley, basil, thyme, marjoram)

Pinch of freshly ground black pepper

1 Heat the oil in a pan set over a medium heat. Add the minced onion and cook for a minute or two, stirring, then add the garlic to the party. Cook for another minute, until the mixture is just beginning to brown, then turn off the heat and set aside.

2 Pulse the beets in a food processor to break them up. Add all the remaining ingredients, including the onion and garlic, and pulse until you have a coarse puree. Taste and adjust the seasoning with a little more lemon juice, herbs, or pepper if needed.

3 You can eat this immediately, but it will keep in the refrigerator for one to two weeks in a sealed container and the flavor actually improves. Just be sure to pour a little olive oil over the top to protect the top from oxidation.

BEET TAPENADE

FIG AND OLIVE TAPENADE

GREEN OLIVE AND PRESERVED LEMON TAPENADE

Lacto-fermented pestos

Pesto comes from the Italian word *pestar*, meaning "to crush" or "to grind." Just think pestle and then start adding your ingredients! The sky's the limit when it comes to all the different variations of pesto you can make beyond basil and pine nuts—think dill, arugula, kale, Thai basil, or even nettle. Bursting with flavor, pesto is the perfect accompaniment to meals and snacks.

Pesto doesn't need to be fermented, but when it is, it increases the shelf life from a week to at least a month, preserving your energy as well as adding all those fantastic friendly little microbes. It's also a great way to use up your leftover brines and kefir whey.

KALE PESTO

Kale has a strong flavor when fermented, so it's a good idea to pair it with other strong flavors.
MAKES 1 X 1/2-PINT JAR

1/2 ounce fresh basil

1/2 ounce kale

1/2 cup walnuts

2 Brazil nuts

2 fermented garlic cloves (page 68)

Juice of 1/2 lemon

4 tablespoons extra virgin olive oil

2 tablespoons fresh whey or pickle brine

1/2 teaspoon Himalayan rock salt or sea salt

Toss everything into a food processor and blend. Transfer to a clean 1/2-pint jar, making sure you leave 1 inch of headspace at the top of the jar. Leave to ferment for two days, then store in the refrigerator for up to one month.

KEFIR PISTACHIO PESTO

Pesto can take many different directions. The kefir labneh cheese not only acts as a wonderful preservative, but it gives it a unique creamy quality too. ***MAKES 1 X 1/2-PINT JAR***

2 garlic cloves

I cup shelled and unsalted roasted pistachios

24 fresh basil leaves, torn into small pieces

4 tablespoons chopped fresh flat-leaf parsley

3 1/2 ounces labneh cheese (page 138) or hard cheese (page 149)

1/2 cup grated Parmesan cheese (or use 2 tablespoons nutritional yeast for a vegan option)

1/2 cup extra virgin olive oil

2 tablespoons freshly squeezed lemon juice

1/2 teaspoon sea salt

1 Place the garlic in a food processor and pulse a few times, until finely minced. Add the pistachios, basil, and parsley and pulse again several times. Add the rest of the ingredients and process until the pesto is well combined. Taste and adjust the seasoning if needed.

2 Serve immediately or store in an airtight container in the refrigerator for one month. Bring to room temperature for 30 minutes before serving so that it's easy to spread.

NASTURTIUM PESTO

Maybe it's because these little bursts of floral beauty are so easy to grow that I love them (I didn't inherit my father's green thumb). Plant a few seeds—they are beyond rewarding as the flower, leaf and seedpod are all edible (try the nasturtium capers on page 55). The peppery taste of the leaves and flowers will surprise you and they'll add a burst of beauty to your plate.

MAKES 1 X 1-PINT JAR

I cup walnuts

I cup grated Parmesan cheese or 5 tablespoons nutritional yeast

4 ounces nasturtium leaves

2 ounces nasturtium flowers

5 garlic cloves, peeled

I cup olive oil

2 tablespoons fresh whey or pickle brine

Toss everything into a food processor and blend. Transfer to a clean pint jar, making sure you leave 1 inch of headspace at the top of the jar. Leave to ferment for two days, then store in the refrigerator for up to one month.

DAIRY AND NUT MILK

FERMENTS

VIILI, MATSONI, PIIMA, filmjölk, ayran, ryazhenka, skyr, kefir. Sound familiar? What about yogurt? They are all essentially the same thing—a cultured dairy product.

The dairy debate is a passionate one with a fascinating history. It's thought that the story began around 7,500 years ago in a region between the central Balkans and central Europe as we domesticated the cow and adapted to its milk due to nutritional needs. This practice spread across the sun-deprived northern regions because of those people's greater need for vitamin D in their diet. One culture that offers a fascinating slant to the debate is the Maasai tribes in Africa, as milk plays a huge role in their diet. They drink what might appear to be an unorthodox mix of cow's milk and cow's blood.

In most cultures milk was not consumed fresh, but rather fermented to make yogurt (note all the cultural variations above!), butter, and cheese. From Turkey to Norway, there are so many different traditional fermented milks to discover.

But let me make something very clear. If I didn't have access to raw organic milk, cow or goat, I would not be consuming milk. For me, every food consideration starts with the story behind it. The subject of milk and whether or not we should drink it is a heated topic with many valid points on the ethics, nutrition, quality, and quantity of milk, and I can appreciate all sides. However, I do wonder if our convenient replacement of milk with alternative milks with the same fanatical level of consumption will result in some interesting studies in years to come. →

Raw milk already comes with its own set of probiotics and enzymes. Culturing it greatly enhances its probiotic and enzyme content, making it a therapeutic food for our digestive system and overall health.

I'm fortunate to have access to a supply of raw milk from Culmore Organic Farm in Kilrea, where David Laughlin keeps a herd that lives in five-star luxury. They have a huge space to call home and lots of room to roam. They also have a 4-inch-thick mattress to sleep on, fluffed up with sawdust and lime, thank you very much. They have their own grooming station, a self-serve rock salt-licking station, and a robotic milking machine, which they choose to go to. Life is pretty stress free. I'd sleep there myself! Less intensive farming means genuinely happy cows, less stress, and less disease. Best yet, he practices prevention and gives his calves a daily dose of kefir to boost their immune system. As far as I can see it's a farming practice to be supported, and as consumers we have a powerful resource in our pockets to support what we believe is ethical and sustainable.

Kefir

If you're interested in addressing the bacterial ecosystem in your gut, one thing that you should definitely consider adding to your diet is kefir. Kefir is a probiotic-like yogurt. It contains strains of beneficial yeast and bacteria in a way that is very nourishing for our bodies. Unlike yogurt, it survives the initial saliva in your mouth and makes it past the stomach and into the gut, rebuilding and fortifying your gut with good probiotics to boost your health. Kefir is also easy to make, unlike yogurt, which requires a sterile environment and strict temperatures. The best milk kefir is made with whole, raw, organic milk, which is a thick, creamy powerhouse.

During fermentation the casein and lactose are broken down, changing the chemical composition of the milk, rendering it relatively low in lactose and casein. If you struggle with lactose or casein but can tolerate butter or yogurt, try adding kefir to your diet in small amounts to begin with.

MILK KEFIR

If your palate is new to fermented and cultured foods, kefir can take a little getting used to. The tang and the tart taste are strong on a tongue more accustomed to sweet, but it can develop into a taste that is soothing and enjoyable. **MAKES 1 X 1-QUART JAR**

4 tablespoons milk kefir grains (see page 26)

4 cups whole raw milk

1 Put the kefir grains in a clean 1-quart jar and fill almost to the top with the milk. Cover with a clean cloth and set aside on your kitchen counter for one to two days, stirring periodically with a wooden spoon—this is particularly important, as metal appears to damage the cultures.

2 After 24 to 48 hours (the most favorable culturing time), strain out the kefir grains with a plastic strainer set over a jug. The grains are then popped back into a clean jar with some new milk and the process continues. In the jug you now have your milk kefir, which you can enjoy as is or in a variety of ways, both sweet and savory. Other wonderful ways to use kefir include in a filling breakfast (page 169), or for see page 333 for a simple kefir cleanse.

CHOCOLATE SMOOTHIE

This one is for adults and kids alike. **SERVES 1**

I cup almond milk
....
$^1\!/_2$ cup milk kefir (page 134)
....
I banana
....
I heaped tablespoon cacao powder
....
I tablespoon oats
....
I tablespoon nut butter
....
Pinch of sea salt

Blend until smooth and enjoy.

GOLDEN SMOOTHIE

CHOCOLATE SMOOTHIE

GOLDEN PASTE

Keep a supply of delicious, health-boosting golden paste, ready to make all manner of things, including the golden smoothie. **MAKES 2¹/₂ OUNCES**

2 ounces fresh turmeric, peeled and chopped, or 3 tablespoons ground turmeric
....
1 ounce fresh ginger, peeled and chopped, or 2 tablespoons ground ginger
....
5 tablespoons coconut oil or almond oil
....
Filtered water

Put the turmeric, ginger, and oil in a blender with enough water to blitz to a smooth paste. This mixture can be kept in a glass jar in the fridge for two weeks or it can be frozen into cubes. I prefer to freeze it in silicone chocolate molds for easy portions.

GOLDEN SMOOTHIE

While I try to stay away from sugar-laden fruit smoothies, they are a wonderful way to hide some hugely beneficial superfoods such as camu camu, lúcuma, and a tasteless powder called diatomaceous earth (food grade). This is especially good for little ones who need a little cleanse every so often. **SERVES 1**

¹/₂ apple
....
2 to 5 dates, to sweeten
....
1 slice of kiwi
....
1 cup milk kefir (page 134)
....
¹/₂ teaspoon (one portion) golden paste
....
Pinch of freshly ground black pepper

Blend until smooth and enjoy.

BASIC KEFIR DRESSING

Kefir is wonderfully versatile and can be used as a savory foundation for creamy dressings.

For the next three recipes, simply mix everything together and adjust the seasoning as desired, then store in the fridge for up to one month.
MAKES 1 CUP

1 cup milk kefir (page 134)

1/2 onion, thinly sliced

4 sun-dried tomatoes, rehydrated and sliced

3 garlic cloves, smashed and sliced

1 teaspoon sea salt

HERBY RANCH-STYLE DRESSING

This recipe can also be made by raiding your herb beds. ***MAKES 1 1/2 CUPS***

1 1/2 cups milk kefir (page 134)

1 teaspoon dried dill

1 teaspoon garlic powder

1 teaspoon onion powder

1/2 teaspoon dried chives

1/2 teaspoon dried parsley

1/2 teaspoon sea salt

1/4 teaspoon freshly ground black pepper

HONEY MUSTARD DRESSING

Experimenting leads to new discoveries, such as this dressing, which will not disappoint. ***MAKES 1 CUP***

1/2 cup extra virgin olive oil

1/4 cup milk kefir (page 134)

4 tablespoons raw apple cider vinegar or kombucha vinegar (page 318)

1 tablespoon Italian seasoning

1 tablespoon raw honey

2 teaspoons fermented mustard (page 112)

CAESAR SALAD-STYLE DRESSING

Xanthan gum is produced by the bacterial fermentation of a sugar-containing medium. It's added to dressings to thicken them if desired.
MAKES 2 CUPS

2 cups milk kefir (page 134)

1 heaped tablespoon finely chopped fresh parsley

1 heaped tablespoon finely chopped fresh chives

1 heaped tablespoon finely chopped garlic

1 heaped tablespoon lemon zest

1 teaspoon sea salt

1/4 teaspoon Herbamare seasoning

1/2 teaspoon xanthan gum

Place all the ingredients except the xanthan gum in a blender and whiz together. Slowly add the xanthan gum and continue to blend until the dressing thickens. The full flavor will develop after six to eight hours at room temperature. Store in the fridge for up to one month.

LABNEH CHEESE

Turning your delicious homemade milk kefir into labneh (strained cheese) couldn't be easier! It's time to throw out the Boursin and get your own goodness on the go. This is not available in any shop.

For me there is something rather comforting in hanging dripping cloths of milk kefir from cupboard handles. It reminds me of my childhood kitchen and the hanging bags of delicious honey filtering through fine muslin.

Labneh cheese can be rolled into small balls, coated with herbs, spices, or dehydrated powders, and stored in olive oil. These delicious little nuggets are equally wonderful to dig into for a quick snack or an elaborate occasion. As a shortcut you can use natural yogurt the same way, or viili, piima, filmjölk . . . you get the idea!

This soft, creamy, spreadable cheese is fantastic served with honey for a phenomenal sweet creamy treat. Or let your imagination run wild with all sorts of mixes and culinary creations. One of my favorites is to mix ½ pound labneh with ¾ cup chopped walnuts (preferably activated—see page 165), three tablespoons of your favorite sweetener (such as palm sugar, date sugar, honey, maple syrup, etc.) and half a teaspoon of ground cinnamon. Or to make a lemon labneh cheese, add the zest of one lemon or half a preserved lemon, finely chopped, to four tablespoons of the plain cheese and stir through.

MAKES ½ POUND

3 cups milk kefir

1 Line a sieve with some cheesecloth or calico cotton and place the sieve over a bowl. Pour your delicious kefir into this set-up, then tie up the cloth, hang it from a cupboard handle, and just let it drip away into a bowl set underneath.

2 Let it drain for eight to 14 hours (overnight is generally a good rule) and you'll have an ultra-soft, smooth, and tangy spread. Straining the kefir for just a couple of hours will give you Greek-style kefir. Leave it for 24 to 48 hours and you have a thicker, firmer labneh, similar to the consistency of cream cheese. If you strain it for even longer—say, 48 to 72 hours—and press it with a weight, you'll get a harder, crumbly cheese. Once it's ready, store your labneh in the fridge and eat within one month.

Sweet healing water

As you delight in your creamy labneh creation, you will notice that what has dripped off is significantly more than what was left behind in the cloth. Yes, you now have whey and are probably wondering what to do with it! Whatever you do, don't throw that whey out.

Sweet whey that is drained from kefir is a very different product from acid whey. Acid whey is the liquid produced from cultured dairy products that use an acid or rennet to separate the milk, such as paneer, feta, and hard cheeses. The list below refers to uses for sweet whey only.

You can make sweet whey from clabbered raw milk (which is raw milk that is left to sour), yogurt, or buttermilk.

- Substitute whey in **any baking recipe** that calls for water or even milk. Add it to cornbread, pancakes, waffles, and muffins.

- You can use whey as **a starter** for fermented vegetables, condiments, sauerkraut, chutneys, jams, etc. Just be aware that using whey results in the vegetable ferments developing a dominance of whey bacteria.

- Use whey to **soak grains** as the acid medium. This traditional technique makes your grains and legumes more digestible.

- **Freeze it** in ice cube trays or portioned cup measurements to use later in your kitchen adventures.

- Use whey to **cook pasta**, potatoes, oatmeal, or rice. Boiling the whey will cause it to lose its raw properties, but if you feel like you are drowning in whey, this is a wonderful way to use it up and add extra flavor to food.

- Add whey to **soups and stews** at the end of the cooking time.

- Add whey to **smoothies**.

- **Make traditional lemonades** with whey. You'll be amazed at how refreshing, fizzy, and delicious these drinks are (see the recipes on page 293). They're my favorite.

- Use whey as a **hair product**! You can mix it with some essential oils if you want to ease your mind that you won't smell like a dairy farm.

- If it's good for you, it's **good for the dogs**. Feed it to your pets and watch their coats start to shine.

- Use whey to **water your plants**—just dilute it with an equal amount of water in a watering can. A small amount is beneficial but too much is detrimental, as is the case with many things!

- If you're a meat eater, **make a whey marinade**. Add your favorite spices and seasonings to the whey and use it to marinate steaks, chicken, fish, or pork chops. The enzymes in the whey help to break down the meat and add flavor.

- If all else fails, **pour it in your compost bin** rather than down the drain.

CULTURED CREAM

It's possible to ferment cream with kefir grains. The process is just as easy as making kefir with milk, but be prepared for a rather thick product after 24 hours of culturing and a little bit of extra time to pass it through a sieve to collect your kefir grains again. One bonus is that the subsequent batch of kefir made with these grains will be extra lush. To save yourself the hassle, though, you can simply add some ready-to-go fermented kefir to your cream and allow it to work its magic for you. **MAKES 1 X ½-PINT JAR**

I cup full-fat cream
....
I tablespoon milk kefir (page 134)

Mix the cream with the milk kefir in a clean ¹/₂-pint jar and allow to culture for 12 to 24 hours at room temperature. When it's done, transfer to the fridge, where it will keep for one month.

KEFIR SOUR CREAM

I love when you discover a shortcut in the kitchen and the precious ferment that you have been nurturing can perform another alchemic trick for you. Milk kefir is a living beverage teeming with good bacteria that can culture cream for you too, turning it into sour cream—it's easy when you know how. You can use this sour cream in many ways, but if you're feeling extra adventurous, you could even make some cultured butter!
MAKES 1 X 1-QUART JAR

I quart heavy cream
....
¹/₄ cup milk kefir (page 134)

Pour the cream into a clean 1-quart jar and inoculate with the kefir, mixing it well. Leave 1 inch of headspace at the top of the jar. Close the lid and let this sit out and ferment overnight, then transfer to the fridge for up to one month.

CULTURED BUTTER

Not that there's really anything inherently wrong with the butter you might find in your grocery store, but sometimes homemade just tastes better.
MAKES ½ CUP

2 cups kefir sour cream (page 142)

I cup ice-cold filtered water

1 Sour your cream as per the recipe on the previous page. Put half of it in a food processor and blend until it separates, then pour off the liquid. This is buttermilk, so set it aside and use it wherever buttermilk is called for in a recipe. The yellow solids that remain are the butter.

2 Pour some cold filtered water in with the butter and process again. This is called washing the butter. Pour off the water and discard it. Repeat with the remaining cream.

3 At this point you can scoop your butter into an airtight container and store it in the fridge, but I prefer to go rustic and make it into rolls. Take a sheet of waxed paper and spread the butter lengthways on it in a rough cylinder shape. Use the paper to roll the butter into a cylinder, then wrap it up in the paper and twist the ends. Chill until firm. To use, just slice off a disc of butter. It will keep for one month in the fridge.

Nut milk kefirs

Because this food is so unbelievably abundant and giving, of course you can ferment your coconut milks and nut milks too. If using the live milk kefir grains, they will need a boost feed of cow or goat milk every few turns, but if animal milk isn't your gig, then these milks will ferment well if you use a probiotic capsule instead.

COCONUT MILK KEFIR

If you are using coconut milk predominantly, then to help maintain the integrity of the kefir grains it will be necessary to rest them in dairy milk for at least 24 hours after making coconut milk kefir three times. This is because they require lactose (milk sugar) in order to thrive.

MAKES 1 X 1-PINT JAR

2 cups coconut milk

2 tablespoons milk kefir grains (see page 26)

1 Place the coconut milk and the milk kefir grains in a clean pint jar. Cover with a cloth and leave at room temperature to culture for at least 12 hours. Taste the kefir after this time—if you're happy with the taste, then it's ready. Otherwise, leave for another 12 hours to develop a more tart taste. Strain out the milk kefir grains and add to new coconut milk to repeat the process.

2 Store the fermented coconut milk kefir in the refrigerator until you drink it. It will keep for one month.

3 You can do a secondary ferment if you want to add more flavor. Secondary fermenting may sound a little complex, but all it really means is flavoring the kefir overnight, usually with some fruit. While the fruit is infusing the milk with its flavor, the live bacteria are happily reducing the sugar load.

NUT MILK KEFIR

Unlike coconut milk, nut milks are not as successful at making kefir, as there simply isn't enough food for the little grains. If you want to culture nut milks for better digestion, I recommend using a probiotic capsule. They predigest the almond milk, making it easier for you to digest. **MAKES ½ GALLON**

I cup raw almonds or any other nut

8 cups filtered water

4 probiotic capsules or I tablespoon probiotic powder

Lemon juice, to taste (optional)

1 Start by soaking your raw almonds in water for eight hours or more in preparation for making the nut milk.

2 Strain the water from the almonds and place in a blender with the 8 cups of filtered water. Blend on high for several minutes. Pour this mixture through a nut milk bag into a glass bowl or jug. Squeeze the remaining liquid through the bag and you are left with a lovely nut milk.

3 Crack open the probiotic capsules, add the powder to your almond milk, and stir gently with a clean spoon. Cover your glass bowl or jug with a paper towel or a clean tea towel and let it sit on the counter at room temperature for 12 hours or overnight to culture. After about 12 hours, the probiotics will have proliferated and multiplied tremendously, leaving you with a super probiotic-rich liquid. There will be a thick layer at the top, which contains the fat content from the almonds, and the bottom layer will be pure liquid. Don't be alarmed—just stir to reincorporate. At this point, you can add a squeeze of lemon juice to suit your taste.

4 Transfer to a clean sealable bottle and store in the fridge for up to one week. Reserving ½ cup of this nut milk kefir will allow you to start the next batch: use two tablespoons of nut milk kefir in place of each probiotic capsule.

Nut cheeses

Nuts are not the easiest foods to digest. They are coated in phytic acid, which is an enzyme inhibitor that essentially preserves them. But when we ferment them we make them a highly digestible probiotic food and a perfect alternative to dairy.

I use cashews, walnuts, Brazil nuts, almonds, and even sunflower seeds in the recipes that follow, but if your budget can stretch to it, macadamia nuts and pine nuts also make fabulous cheeses that are rich, creamy, and well-balanced in flavor.

What ignites the nut mixture to ferment? I like to use fermented vegetables because I always have some on hand. Plus they're healthy and flavorful and their moisture helps the blender to run smoothly. You can also add probiotic powder to the mix. You can get it at a health food store and it comes as a powder, tablets, or in capsules.

BROWN RICE CRACKERS

HARD CHEESE ROLLED IN
DUKKAH AND HERBS

SOFT CHEESE

SOAKED OATS BREAD   LEMONY HUMMUS

SOFT CHEESE

There are a few options when it comes to texture for your cheeses. One is this hummus-like texture. It's the fastest, easiest method and makes a mean sandwich spread. **MAKES 1 POUND**

2 cups sunflower seeds, macadamia nuts, or pine nuts

5 ounces fermented vegetables

I garlic clove, smashed and chopped

2 tablespoons extra virgin coconut oil or olive oil

I tablespoon nutritional yeast

I tablespoon freshly squeezed lemon juice

$^1/_2$ teaspoon sea salt

1 Place the seeds or nuts in a bowl, cover with cold water, and soak overnight.

2 The next day, drain the seeds or nuts and place in a blender with the fermented veggies, garlic, oil, nutritional yeast, and lemon juice. Blend until smooth, then season to taste with the salt. Transfer to a bowl, cover with a cloth, and allow to culture for 24 hours at room temperature.

3 At this point, the cheese is ready to eat. If you want a thicker cheese spread, line a sieve with cheesecloth and set the sieve over a bowl to collect the liquid as it drains. Put the blended cheese mixture into the cheesecloth and hang it up for a few hours to allow some moisture to drip away. It will keep for one week in the fridge.

HARD CHEESE

This cheese is firm enough to slice with a knife. **MAKES 1 POUND**

I cup raw almonds

I cup filtered water

I teaspoon light miso

$1/2$ teaspoon probiotic powder

2 tablespoons nutritional yeast flakes

$1/2$ teaspoon garlic powder

$1/2$ teaspoon sea salt

$1/8$ teaspoon ground nutmeg

I teaspoon organic cold-pressed flax oil

1 Place the almonds in a bowl, cover with cold water, and soak for eight to ten hours, then drain, rinse, and remove their skins.

2 Put the soaked, skinned almonds in a blender with the 1 cup filtered water, miso, and probiotic powder. Blend until smooth.

3 Line a colander with a cheesecloth or some calico cotton and set over a bowl. Put the blended cheese mixture into the cloth and cover with the overhanging edges of the cloth. Place a small plate and weight on top. The bowl will collect any liquid as it drains. Leave to drain and ferment in a warm place for 12 to 24 hours.

4 Once fermented, mix the nutritional yeast, garlic powder, salt, and nutmeg together in a large bowl, then add the flax oil and the strained cheese and mix until well combined.

5 Press into molds (such as a small cake pan) and refrigerate for at least four hours. You can coat these wheels of cheese in whatever takes your fancy: try cracked black pepper and coarse salt, herbs, or some other dehydrated seasoning. (If you want to create a rind, place them in a dehydrator at 100°F for six hours.) Wrap in parchment paper and store in the fridge for five to six days.

SOAKED OATS BREAD

EASY FETA-STYLE CHEESE

CHEESE LOG

You can have a lot of fun flavoring your cheeses with lemon zest, herbs, olives, harissa, or asafetida powder, then rolling it in fresh or dried herbs, kraut or kimchi dust (page 334), or nettle seeds.

MAKES 1 POUND

2 cups Brazil nuts

5 ounces fermented vegetables

1 garlic clove, smashed and chopped

1/2 cup filtered water

1/4 cup olive oil

2 tablespoons sesame oil (preferably black sesame oil)

1 tablespoon extra virgin coconut oil

1 tablespoon tamari or liquid aminos

1 tablespoon chopped fresh ginger

1 tablespoon finely chopped dulse

1 teaspoon high-quality miso

Make as outlined in the hard cheese recipe on page 149, diverging when it requires you to press it into molds. You can simply transfer your "cheese" mixture into a sheet of parchment paper and roll it into a log shape. This is a good opportunity to coat it in the wonderful blends mentioned in the introduction. The cheese will be quite firm due to the oils added and will keep in the fridge for two weeks.

EASY FETA-STYLE CHEESE

For a little indulgence, treat yourself to a macadamia cheese at least once. If you're using this recipe to make The Cultured Club's celebration chocolate cake on page 273, use cashews instead of macadamia nuts, omit the yeast, and skip step 3 altogether.

MAKES 1 POUND

2 cups macadamia nuts

1 cup filtered water

1 teaspoon probiotic powder

2 teaspoons nutritional yeast

3/4 teaspoon sea salt

1 Place the nuts in a bowl, cover with cold water, and soak for four hours. Drain the water off and transfer the nuts to a blender.

2 Blend the nuts, filtered water, and probiotic powder in a high-speed blender until smooth. Place in a sieve lined with a cheesecloth and press as in the hard cheese on page 149, applying a weight that's heavy enough to press it down but not so heavy as to press the cheese out of the cloth. Leave to culture for 24 hours at room temperature. Once cultured, stir in the nutritional yeast and salt.

3 Spread the mixture onto some parchment paper in a layer about 1/2-inch thick. Season if desired (see the introduction to the cheese log recipe for ideas). Cover with another sheet of parchment paper and place in the fridge to firm up. To serve, cut the cheese into small cubes. It will keep for one week in the fridge.

BREADS AND CRACKERS

I HAVEN'T ENJOYED bread in more than five years. In that time I have tried, as the smell of freshly baked bread still makes me salivate. But as my palate has changed due to increasing the quantity of fermented foods in my diet, I no longer enjoy the sweet, doughy taste or texture of this food and it's a feat to digest it. However, my family love bread and are able to eat it. Give my children a slice of white bread and they won't believe their luck. The only type of bread we should be eating is either one that's made from sprouted flour or a sourdough, as the high level of phytates in the bread are reduced when you have sprouted or fermented the flour.

Ideally, we should gather as our scobies do—to form a group of people with a common interest, like a club, each person specializing in the different ferments we wish to include in our diet, then swapping and trading our prized creations. Keeping a sourdough starter can become a serious side project as you practice making a perfect loaf of bread. It can be really challenging to keep the sourdough starter alive, feed the kefir, change the kombucha, make the kraut, eat the kimchi . . . you get the idea. That's why my husband looks after the sourdough starter. So if it all starts to feel a little overwhelming, find another fermentation fanatic and start trading!

SOAKED OATS BREAD

This recipe comes from Sarah Britton's My New Roots blog, where she calls it Life-Changing Loaf of Bread. I just couldn't resist making it as a fermented version with the addition of kefir or whey instead of water. **MAKES 1 LOAF**

I¹/₂ cups rolled oats
....
I cup sunflower seeds
....
¹/₂ cup flaxseeds
....
¹/₂ cup hazelnuts or almonds
....
4 tablespoons psyllium husks or 3 tablespoons psyllium husk powder
....
2 tablespoons chia seeds
....
I teaspoon fine sea salt or I¹/₂ teaspoons coarse salt
....
I¹/₂ cups liquid (kefir or I part whey diluted with I part filtered water)
....
3 tablespoons melted coconut oil or ghee
....
I tablespoon maple syrup or raw honey

1 Combine all the dry ingredients in a large mixing bowl, stirring well. I prefer to mill the dry ingredients like a rough flour.

2 Mix the liquid, oil, and maple syrup together in a small bowl. Add the wet ingredients to the dry ingredients and mix very well until everything is completely soaked and the dough is thick.

3 Line a standard loaf pan with parchment paper and scrape the ingredients into the pan, pressing it down well. Let this sit out on the counter overnight.

4 The next day, preheat the oven to 350°F.

5 Place the loaf pan in the oven on the middle rack and bake for 20 minutes. Remove the bread from the pan. Place it upside down directly on the oven rack and bake for another 30 to 40 minutes, until the bread sounds hollow when you tap it. Let it cool completely before slicing. This keeps for five days in the fridge and it freezes well too.

WHOLEGRAIN KEFIR SPELT BREAD

This is a quick soaked bread that uses milk kefir, as I'm expecting you to have that on the go at this stage. **MAKES 2 LOAVES**

6 cups wholegrain spelt flour

3 cups milk kefir (page 134)

2 tablespoons melted coconut oil or butter

I tablespoon raw honey

I teaspoon aluminium-free baking soda

Butter or coconut oil, for greasing

1 Mix the flour and kefir together in a large bowl. It might be hard to stir, so you may want to knead it. Let this sit overnight, covered with a clean tea towel.

2 The next day, add the melted coconut oil, honey, and baking soda to the dough and mix well. Cover loosely and put in a warm place to rise for about four hours.

3 Preheat the oven to 350°F. Generously grease two standard loaf pans with butter or coconut oil.

4 Divide the dough in half. Shape into two loaves and place in the greased pans.

5 Bake for 30 minutes, until the loaves sound hollow when you tap them on the bottom.

FLAXSEED FOCACCIA À LA SUSAN JANE WHITE

My life is a better life having encountered Susan Jane White and her fabulous recipes in general. Although this bread isn't fermented, I've included it because the sweet undertones balance so well with any kind of fermented food piled on top. Plus it's extra kind on your gut, which is what we're all about! It's worth noting that this recipe is not only foolproof, but also hugely flexible. You can play around with the herbs or sub chopped olives for the raisins, for example.

Also, buying whole seeds and milling your own will save you a pretty penny. Radical home economics, remember? ***MAKES 1 LARGE TRAY OR 2 SMALLER STANDARD LOAVES***

2 cups milled flaxseeds or linseeds

3 teaspoons dried rosemary

$^1/_2$ teaspoon baking powder

3 large eggs (or use $^1/_4$ cup aquafaba for a vegan option)

$^3/_4$ cup milk or plant milk

Zest and juice of $^1/_2$ unwaxed lemon

4 tablespoons extra virgin olive oil

2 tablespoons blackstrap molasses

Handful of golden raisins, mulberries, or chopped-up olives (optional)

Flaky smoked sea salt, for sprinkling

1 Preheat the oven to 350°F. Line a 8-by-10-inch pan or two standard loaf pans with parchment paper.

2 Mix the milled seeds with two teaspoons of the rosemary and the baking powder. In a separate bowl, whisk together the eggs, milk, lemon zest and juice, olive oil, and molasses, then stir in the raisins, mulberries, or olives, if using.

3 Add the wet ingredients to the bowl of dry ingredients and mix well to combine. Spread this mix evenly into the pan(s), then sprinkle the remaining teaspoon of rosemary on top along with a pinch of yummy smoked sea salt flakes.

4 Bake for about 25 minutes, then remove from the oven and the pan and transfer to a wire rack. Allow to cool for 25 minutes before slicing.

VEGETABLE BREAD SLICES

Loosely masquerading as a bread, use this in any of the sandwich ideas on page 200. **MAKES 1 TRAY**

1/2 head of cauliflower, broken into florets

I parsnip, peeled and roughly chopped

1 1/4 cups ground almonds

2 tablespoons psyllium husks

3 eggs or 2/3 cup aquafaba

1 Preheat the oven to 390°F. Line a baking tray with parchment paper.

2 Process the cauliflower and parsnip in a food processor until it resembles rice. Transfer to a bowl and add the ground almonds and psyllium husks, then stir in the eggs or aquafaba to form a wet dough.

3 Scrape into the lined baking tray and flatten it out evenly. Place in the oven and bake for 25 minutes, until golden. Allow to cool on a wire rack before cutting into slices and tucking in. This bread is great served with hummus and extra toppings.

GONE CRACKERS

I have gone crackers for crackers. Where bread left a huge gap, it was quickly filled with crackers. They satisfy both in texture and taste like bread never did. To be honest, if it was nutritionally acceptable to eat these crackers all day long, smeared with dips, cheese spreads, and slathered with fermented salsa, I would be delighted. They tickle every taste bud. **MAKES 12 CRACKERS**

1 1/2 cups flour (plain, whole wheat, fresh ground, almond or gluten-free flour all work well), plus extra for dusting

1/4 teaspoon onion powder

1/4 teaspoon garlic powder

4 tablespoons butter or coconut oil

1/4 cup filtered water (add an extra 1/4 cup if you're using gluten-free or almond flour)

I tablespoon raw honey

Flaky sea salt, for sprinkling on top

1 Preheat the oven to 390°F. Lightly dust a baking tray with flour.

2 Measure out the flour, onion powder, and garlic powder into a large mixing bowl. Rub in the butter or oil until it forms pea-sized clumps. Add the water and honey and stir until just combined.

3 Lightly dust your countertop with flour and roll the dough out on it until it's 1/4-inch thick. Use a pizza cutter or cookie cutter to cut into your desired shapes, then place on the baking tray and sprinkle with sea salt.

4 Bake for 10 minutes, until golden. Once cooled, store in an airtight container for up to one week.

FERMENTED FLAXSEED AND
ONION CRACKERS

BUCKWHEAT
CRACKERS

BROWN RICE
CRACKERS

FERMENTED FLAXSEED AND ONION CRACKERS

People can need some encouragement to get across the barrier of tasting fermented foods, and when I teach these lost traditions, that's a huge part of the learning. We need to register the memory on our palates, as it's one that has been lost.

And when people do try them, they are genuinely surprised that they taste so good. These crackers get the most attention and are the most requested recipe. While they are generally never the same twice, the foundation of the cracker doesn't change. I'll use whatever I have around me when I make them—I love to hide my ferments in these. The ends of jars of sauerkraut that have lost their charm are a great addition. You can even intentionally plop a whole jar of fermented onions in here or a generous quantity of fermented garlic or both, keeping all the deliciousness and probiotics intact. These crackers allow for total experimentation and the results have yet to fail. Adding greens like collard and kale boosted with spirulina powder and dulse flakes is highly encouraged too.

The most successful crackers are made in a dehydrator, but I realize not everyone has one so I've included an option to make them in the oven too.

MAKES 1 TRAY

¹/₂ cup sunflower seeds

¹/₂ cup ground flaxseeds

¹/₂ cup almonds or your nut of choice

Coconut oil, for greasing

¹/₂ cup old-fashioned rolled oats or quinoa flakes (optional)

1 x ¹/₂-pint jar of fermented onions (page 67)

2 tablespoons olive oil

2 tablespoons tamari

1 teaspoon dried thyme

1 teaspoon dried rosemary

FOR THE TOPPING (OPTIONAL):

Poppy seeds

Nigella seeds

White or black sesame seeds (or both)

Sunflower seeds

Fresh herbs

1 Soak the flaxseeds in a bowl of cold water overnight. Place the nuts, sunflower seeds, and oats in a separate bowl and soak overnight as well.

2 The next day, preheat the oven to 340°F if you aren't using a dehydrator. Line a baking tray with parchment paper and grease the paper with coconut oil.

3 Drain and rinse the soaked sunflower seeds, nuts, and oats, then place in a food processor and pulse until the almonds and oats are a lumpy paste, but don't over-process. Drain and rinse the soaked flaxseeds, then add them to the food processor along with the olive oil, tamari, fermented onions, and spices and blend again to form a smooth, gloopy batter.

4 To make these in the oven, spread the batter onto the lined and greased tray in a layer about $\frac{1}{4}$-inch thick. If you like, sprinkle with seeds and/ or any herb you fancy, pressing any additional ingredients into the batter. Score the mix before baking so it's easy to snap your cooked crackers apart.

5 Bake for 3 hours. Flip the crackers over after this time if you wish and continue to bake for another two to three hours, until the crackers are as crisp as you would like.

6 Alternatively, if you're using a dehydrator, spread this batter onto Teflex sheets in a layer about $\frac{1}{4}$-inch thick. Dehydrate at 110°F for four to six hours, then flip onto the mesh, removing the Teflex sheet. Continue to dehydrate overnight.

7 The crackers will keep in an airtight container for many months, but I'm not exactly sure because they have never lasted long enough for me to find out.

BROWN RICE CRACKERS

These crackers are a simple variation on my house staple of flaxseed crackers on the previous page. The deep umami flavor of these is a nice addition to a simple, quick snack. **MAKES 2 TRAYS**

3 tablespoons flaxseeds

¹/₂ cup filtered water or brine

²/₃ cup cooked brown rice

¹/₂ cup sesame seeds

I ounce seaweed kraut (page 38)

3 sheets of nori

3 heaped tablespoons bonito flakes

I tablespoon tamari

I tablespoon olive oil

I teaspoon to I tablespoon sea salt, to taste

1 Preheat the oven to 325°F.

2 Soak the flaxseeds in the water or brine for 15 minutes.

3 Blitz all the ingredients together in a food processor until sticky and fully mixed together, including the flaxseeds and the water or brine you soaked them in. If it's not sticky, add a splash more water.

4 Spread out the mixture on two pieces of parchment paper as thinly and evenly as you can, or place between two sheets of parchment paper and roll it out until it's very thin, then remove the top piece of paper. Use a sharp knife to make score lines for the size of the cracker you want.

5 Transfer the baking paper onto two baking trays and bake in the oven for about 30 minutes, until completely dry. Slice while hot, as they crisp up fast. Store in an airtight tin for four days—if they last that long!

BUCKWHEAT CRACKERS

The joys of buckwheat never end, and turning it into a cracker allows buckwheat's unusual buttery side to shine. These crackers are wide open for experimenting with, adding your flavors, ferments, and superfoods of choice. I love any opportunity to add a little bit of flavor and spice, and this recipe is a great way to tease the palate. **MAKES 2 TRAYS**

$3/4$ pound buckwheat groats, soaked and sprouted

$1/4$ cup almonds, sunflower seeds, and/or pumpkin seeds, soaked and rinsed

$1/4$ cup golden flaxseeds, soaked

1 cup filtered water

3 tablespoons nutritional yeast

2 tablespoons lemon juice

2 tablespoons extra virgin olive oil

2 teaspoons ground cumin

1 teaspoon sea salt

$1/2$ teaspoon ground turmeric

$1/2$ teaspoon paprika

$1/2$ teaspoon chili flakes

7 tablespoons golden flaxseeds, milled

1 Combine all the ingredients in a food processor except the milled flaxseeds and blend until smooth. Add the milled flax and blend again. Allow the mixture to sit and thicken for about ten minutes.

2 Spread the mixture $1/4$-inch thick on Teflex sheets and dehydrate for eight hours at 100°F. Flip onto the mesh, removing the Teflex sheet, and continue to dehydrate for another 12 hours. Break or cut into crackers and store in an airtight container for many months.

Soaking, souring, and sprouting

It's time to start cooking like Granny did and address certain phobias regarding our food. Since adopting the practice of soaking grains, pulses, seeds, and nuts, I have enjoyed a much better digestive system and I now have a completely different palate too. If you are adopting a whole food diet, then soaking is a crucial step that you can't afford to skip.

A seed (or grain or legume) has many nutritional advantages for you, but many of them are locked up tight by anti-nutrients. Once you start the germinating process, though, that dormant seed starts to become a living plant. By soaking grains, also known as culturing, you are helping to break down the anti-nutrients and the harder-to-digest components of the grain while at the same time helping to release highly beneficial nutrients. Soaking does all that hard work so your body doesn't have to. Sounds like a win-win!

The anti-nutrient I'm referring to is phytic acid. It binds with calcium, magnesium, iron, copper, and zinc, making it very difficult for you to absorb nutrients. Consuming high levels of phytates can result in mineral deficiencies, leading to poor bone health and tooth decay as the body leeches calcium from your bones. Phytates will also have a bad effect on your hormone system, they lower metabolism, and contribute to anemia, so really, it's a no-brainer—you need to get rid of it!

Acid mediums are a vital part of the process. The acid is a catalyst to initiate the culturing/fermenting process that enables the enzyme phytase to be released and break down the phytates. Thankfully, it's easy and there are a few options you can use.

Dairy-based acid mediums are whey, whole milk kefir, or cultured buttermilk. Non-dairy acid mediums are lemon juice, raw apple cider vinegar, coconut milk kefir, or water kefir. Plus you only need a little bit. The general ratio is one teaspoon of acid medium to 1 cup warm filtered water.

Soaking usually only takes 12 to 24 hours. I like to see it as an overnight activity. Beyond that, fermentation begins, which is an even more complete way to predigest the grain and neutralize anti-nutrients.

SOAKING

- **Soaking a flour:** Most flour is high in phytase (the enzyme). Get that pancake mix started the night before, just like Granny did!

- **Whole grains:** Simply soak the grains overnight in enough water to cover them along with some acid medium.

- **Oats** contain a large amount of hard-to-digest phytates and other anti-nutrients. Unfortunately, oats are so low in phytase that something high in phytase is best added to the soak to help, like one tablespoon of buckwheat groats along with your water and acid mix.

- **Nuts and seeds** need to soak in warm salt water for approximately seven hours. You can dehydrate them afterward to make crispy nuts, the flavor of which is incomparable to what you currently know. Nuts that have been soaked and then dehydrated are referred to as activated nuts. The soaking process removes the phytic acid that coats them, while dehydrating them removes any moisture that would cause them to spoil. This helps to make the nuts more digestible and less likely to cause intestinal discomfort. Additionally, roasting most likely helps to further remove phytic acid, but you do lose some of the nutritional benefits of the nut.

- **Beans and legumes:** The traditional method for preparing beans is to soak them in hot water (not boiling) for at least 12 to 24 hours, changing the soaking water at least once during this time.

SOURING

- Souring refers to the **process of fermentation**. Sourdough is probably the most widely known method of grain fermentation. Some of the traditional pancake batters mentioned on page 224 use this process. Souring is a book in its own right!

SPROUTING

- In the simplest terms, sprouting is the **process of seed germination**. In the case of grains, the grain "seed" is kept warm and damp, just as it would be in the soil, and after a short period of time a tiny sprout begins to emerge from the very core of the grain.

- Grains can be **sprouted in large batches** and **dried for storage**. They can then be ground into flour as needed and made into bread without the need for soaking or souring afterwards.

- Sprouting is also a good way to **prepare whole grains** that will be consumed as a side dish.

SOAKED BREAKFASTS

THERE ARE MANY breakfasts to indulge in, but for me it has to be porridge. It is one meal I shall never give up on and I will not give in to the cereal alternatives. Luckily, the whole family is happy with that . . . for now!

These breakfast ideas using soaking principles actually make your morning stress free, as they don't take long to prepare (see pages 164–165 for notes on soaking). Bigger projects, like making the buckwheat crispies, can be saved for the weekend as an investment for the week ahead, as they store well.

Oats contain the highest amount of phytic acid of any grain, so proper preparation is important. Phytic acid binds with calcium, magnesium, iron, copper, and zinc, making it very difficult for you to absorb nutrients, but soaking grains reduces their phytic acid, which can make them easier to digest. Plus soaking them the night before means quicker cooking times, or indeed no cooking at all, allowing you to enjoy the food raw. So join the porridge party!

Soaking does sometimes make your kitchen look like a culinary demo is about to take place any minute, but it has been one of the most beneficial practices alongside fermenting that I have implemented in my kitchen routine by far. In my house, you'll often find a bowl of seeds, a bowl of rice, some kind of pulse, and a grain being put to bed in a bowl of water with a splash of whey or raw apple cider vinegar, just to help the process along.

PORRIDGE

Oats don't naturally contain gluten, but most commercial oat products on the market have been cross-contaminated with wheat, barley, and/or rye during harvesting, transportation, storage, milling, processing, and packaging. Only bags labeled gluten-free will be wheat- or gluten-free.

A wonderful way to experiment with your porridge is to make a big jar of your favorite porridge ingredients by combining them all together: think oats with buckwheat, millet, quinoa, chia seeds, pumpkin seeds, or nuts. Store them all together as a ready-to-go mix. **SERVES 2**

¹/₄ pound rolled oats
I tablespoon buckwheat groats
I tablespoon whey, raw apple cider vinegar, lemon juice, or milk kefir (page 134) (this is your acid medium)
I cup filtered water

1 Soak the oats, buckwheat groats, and acid medium overnight in the filtered water (the groats help with the soaking).

2 The next morning, warm the oats with a little extra water, nut milk, etc. and flavor as you like. For example, cook with some banana and cinnamon for a creamy sweet porridge or grate in some apple for something with a little more texture. I love to top my porridge with an ever-changing mix of fresh berries, tahini, raw honey, bee pollen, cacao nibs, goji berries, toasted coconut flakes, maca powder, maple sugar, kefir, or toasted walnuts and seeds.

OVERNIGHT OATS

For more of a summertime porridge, you can simply soak the oats overnight and eat them cold, straight from the fridge. **MAKES 1 X 1-PINT JAR**

¹/₂ cup rolled oats
¹/₂ cup filtered water or milk
I to 2 tablespoons chia seeds
3 to 4 tablespoons chopped fruit of your choice

Pour the oats into a clean pint jar, then top up with water or your milk of choice. Add the chia seeds and top with fruit. Place the jar in the fridge and allow to soak overnight.

Some wonderful variations to enjoy:
• Blueberries and maple sugar
• Applesauce, activated almonds (page 165), and coconut sugar
• Apricot, crystallized ginger, almonds, and cardamom

KEFIR BREAKFAST

I love a breakfast that's ready to go straight out of the fridge. For an easily digestible option, add the kefir the night before. The beneficial Lactobacilli *in the kefir or yogurt breaks down the starches and sugars in the oats, creating lactic acid (lots of good bacteria). If you have a slow metabolism, try this breakfast to start your day.* **SERVES 1**

5 to 7 fleshy prunes

2 tablespoons oat flakes or oatmeal

I tablespoon ground flaxseed

I teaspoon cacao powder

I¼ cup milk kefir (page 134) or low-fat yogurt

1 Prepare your breakfast in the evening for the next day. Pour some boiling water (about ½ cup) over the prunes. Cover and leave for five to ten minutes.

2 Meanwhile, mix together the oat flakes, flaxseed, and cacao in a bowl, then stir in the kefir. Drain the prunes and chop them finely, adding them to the oats. Mix well and put in the fridge overnight.

3 The next morning, take it out of the fridge and enjoy your breakfast.

GREEN PORRIDGE WITH BUCKWHEAT, CHIA, AND COCONUT

When I travel, I love seeing how humble dishes can be transformed. I brought home this recipe from Australia. It's fun to explore the many different options of grains. This recipe inspired me so much that it became my breakfast of choice every day for about three weeks after I returned. It's nutritionally dense and satisfying. **SERVES 4**

1³/₄ ounces rolled oats

1³/₄ ounces buckwheat groats

¹/₄ cup pumpkin seeds

2 tablespoons whey, raw apple cider vinegar, lemon juice, or milk kefir (page 134) (this is your acid medium)

1 banana, chopped

6 tablespoons chia seeds

²/₃ cup coconut flakes

2 tablespoons goji berries

1 cardamom pod (seeds only)

Filtered water or milk of your choice, for cooking

2 to 3 tablespoons moringa powder

TO SERVE:

Maple syrup or coconut sugar

Bee pollen

Flaxseed oil

Cacao nibs

Hemp seeds

1 Soak your porridge oats, buckwheat groats, and pumpkin seeds in a pot overnight with the acid medium.

2 In the morning, add the chopped banana, chia seeds, coconut flakes, goji berries, and cardamom seeds to the pot along with some extra water or milk. Cook over a low heat until creamy, then stir in the moringa powder.

3 Serve in a bowl and sweeten with maple syrup or coconut sugar if you like. Top with bee pollen, flaxseed oil, cacao nibs, and/or hemp seeds.

RICE AND MISO BREAKFAST

If you're eager to experiment with a nutritious, warm, filling and savory/sweet breakfast, then give this one a go. If you have leftover rice, it could be worked into a similar breakfast. **SERVES 2**

³/₄ cup brown rice
¹/₃ cup quinoa
¹/₂ teaspoon ground cinnamon
2 bananas, peeled and sliced ¹/₂-inch thick
2 to 4 tablespoons raw cane sugar, maple syrup, or runny raw honey
2 teaspoons miso
1¹/₄ cups unsweetened coconut milk

1 Soak your rice and quinoa overnight in separate bowls.

2 In the morning, drain and rinse the rice and place in a pot with 2 cups water and the cinnamon and bring to a boil. Cook over a rapid simmer with a lid on for 15 to 25 minutes, until it's almost cooked through but still has a little bite to it. If the rice sticks because the water has all been absorbed, add a little extra hot water.

3 Drain and rinse the quinoa and cook in a separate pot by bringing 4 cups of water to a boil. Add the quinoa, reduce the heat and simmer for 15 minutes, uncovered, until cooked. Drain into a sieve.

4 Once the rice is almost cooked, stir in the bananas, sugar, and miso, then stir in half of the coconut milk and bring back to a boil. Simmer for another ten minutes with the lid off until the rice is fully cooked, stirring frequently. Mix in the quinoa and taste, adding a little more sweetener if needed.

5 To serve, ladle into two bowls, pouring on the remaining coconut milk.

BUCKWHEAT CRISPIES

*These cacao crispies are my healthy adult cereal. I make them in a huge batch and dehydrate them. They are only worth doing if you have a dehydrator. Trying to do them in an oven is not pretty and will not give you the crispy crunch we're after. You can omit the cacao powder and add two or three more tablespoons ground cinnamon and one tablespoon of ground cardamom instead. **MAKES 1 X ½-GALLON JAR***

I pound buckwheat groats

I cup sunflower seeds

I cup pumpkin seeds

3 apples, peeled and sliced

10 dates, pitted

½ cup orange juice or filtered water

I¼ cups cacao powder

3 tablespoons lemon juice

2 tablespoons ground cinnamon

2 teaspoons vanilla extract

I teaspoon sea salt

1 Soak and sprout the buckwheat until you see little tails. This can take two to three days and it's important to rinse it twice a day to avoid any spoilage.

2 When the buckwheat is nearly ready, soak the sunflower seeds and pumpkin seeds overnight, then drain and rinse.

3 Now you're ready to combine everything. Place the apples, dates, and orange juice in a high-speed blender and blend to a paste. Add the soaked seeds, cacao powder, lemon juice, cinnamon, vanilla, and salt and continue to blend until smooth.

4 Transfer the paste into a bowl with the sprouted buckwheat and mix thoroughly. Spread this mix in clusters onto the mesh of your dehydrator trays. It should be quite sticky and not too watery. Allow it to dehydrate for 12 hours at 110°F, until crispy. Transfer to an airtight container and store for up to six months.

5 Serve with your favorite homemade nut milk—hemp milk is good for this particular breakfast.

SOUPS

FROM THE BEGINNING of time (well, at least since man discovered fire), humans all over the world have been boiling bones to glean every last bit of goodness after eating all the meat.

Broth is an integral part of traditional cooking and a waste-free kitchen. There is a lot of goodness in the bones, which are full of valuable, easily digestible nutrients. Broth is making a huge comeback as gut-healing diets highlight how it soothes and heals the gut lining. Regularly consuming broth is a valuable habit that offers benefits for everyone's health. It's wonderful as the foundation for a soup, but you can also use it to cook meats or vegetables, to make sauces with, or just pour some into a cup and sip away!

Broth is one of those foods that you simply must make at home. Commercial broth is a pale imitation of homemade broth, but luckily it's simple enough to make. Generally, in my house we make vegetable broth, though sometimes there will be chicken broth to make the most of a cooked chicken carcass. You can also make a broth with a raw chicken carcass—ask your butcher for this. Either way, I would only consider making broth with an organic, free-range chicken. Bonus for knowing the farmer.

When you make broth, you are extracting as much goodness out of the ingredients as possible and presenting them as minerals that are easy to digest. Using organic produce or meat ensures no synthetic chemicals have been used and the animal has been raised on feed that has not been altered through genetic engineering. In Belfast, we are lucky to have Mullan's Organic Farm from Limavady, who bring their produce the weekly St. George's market.

CHICKEN BROTH

I make this for my children as culinary ammunition in the winter. Broth contains important minerals, such as calcium, magnesium, phosphorus, silicon, sulfur, and trace minerals, in a form that is easy for the body to absorb. Better yet, I can hide it in their food!

MAKES 1/2 GALLON

I to 2 chicken carcasses from previously cooked chickens
....
Filtered water
....
2 tablespoons raw apple cider vinegar

1 Put your chicken carcasses into a large stockpot and cover with filtered water. Depending on how concentrated you want your stock to be, you can fill the pot to the top or only put in enough water to cover the chickens. Add the apple cider vinegar to the pot. This will help remove minerals from the bones. Allow the pot to sit out at room temperature for 30 to 60 minutes.

2 Bring the pot to a boil and remove any scum that rises to the top. Turn the heat down so that the water is just barely simmering and cover with a lid. Check the broth periodically to make sure it's simmering at the proper temperature. If you put a smaller amount of water in your pot, also check to make sure that there is always enough water to cover the bones.

3 Cook the broth for up to 24 hours. A longer cooking time makes more flavorful broth and extracts more nutrition from the bones. When your broth is done cooking, turn off the heat and allow the broth to cool a bit, then strain it into another pot to remove the bones.

4 Pour the broth into heat-safe containers and store in the fridge. If you're not going to eat the broth within five days or so, pour it into freezer-safe containers and store in the freezer. Making a large batch and freezing it in handy ice cube portions is always a good idea.

5 After making your first batch of broth you can reuse the bones to make a second batch.

KITCHEN SCRAPS VEGETABLE STOCK

Onion peels, herb stems and roots, spring onion greens, mushroom stems, carrot peels and celery leaves are all good things to throw into the pot. As a kitchen waste ninja, I freeze kitchen scraps as I go along to build up a sufficient quantity to make a stock. Here is a basic recipe, but add what you have saved.

MAKES 1 QUART

I tablespoon olive oil

3 carrots, chopped

3 celery stalks, chopped

2 large onions, chopped

I to 2 garlic cloves, minced

8 cups filtered water

Frozen vegetable scraps (2 to 3 cups is a good amount)

2 bay leaves

A few sprigs of fresh parsley

A few sprigs of fresh thyme

1 Heat the olive oil in a large pot set over a medium heat. Add the carrots, celery, onions, and garlic. Cook for about five minutes, stirring often, until softened. Add the water, frozen vegetable scraps, bay leaves, parsley, and thyme. Reduce the heat to low and simmer, partially covered, for 45 minutes.

2 Pour the broth through a fine-mesh strainer into a large heatproof bowl or pot. Discard the solids. Once the broth has cooled, transfer it to airtight plastic containers or freezer bags and store it in the freezer for up to six months. Freeze it in 2-cup portions for handiness.

SUPER QUICK JAPANESE DASHI (SEAWEED STOCK)

This broth using kombu seaweed is a great substitute for vegetable or chicken broth in most recipes. For the true Japanese experience (and the non-vegetarian variation), you can omit the tamari, mirin, and sugar and add bonito flakes (which are flakes of dried fish). Serve as is or add some tamari, miso, sea salt or Himalayan salt, and cayenne pepper. It's umami in a bowl.

You can also use the leftover seaweed to make a delicious seaweed relish (see the next page) to serve with a rice bowl. ***MAKES 1 QUART***

4 cups filtered water

³/₄ ounce wakame

¹/₂ ounce kombu, cut into 3-inch pieces

5 tablespoons tamari or liquid aminos (optional)

2 teaspoons raw cane sugar

1 Bring the water to a boil in a large pot set over a high heat. Remove from the heat, then add the mirin, wakame, kombu, tamari, if using, and sugar.

2 Cool completely, then strain, reserving the solids for the seaweed relish on the next page. The dashi can be refrigerated for several days or frozen for up to six months.

SEAWEED RELISH

I love to make a seaweed accompaniment to dishes. Simply hydrating a dried seaweed mix in lemon juice usually suffices. But because it would pain me enormously to discard the cooked seaweed from a dashi, it must be given a second chance. This relish will not disappoint. In fact, you will want to make dashi every day just to make more relish. It is rather special. **SERVES 2**

1 ounce kombu/wakame mix from making the dashi on page 180
....
1 cup filtered water
....
3 tablespoons tamari
....
2 tablespoons raw cane sugar or xylitol
....
2 tablespoons mirin
....
1 teaspoon dashi

1 Drain the kombu from the dashi and slice into thin pieces. Place it in a pan with the water and bring it to a boil, then reduce to a simmer and cook on a low heat for about one hour.

2 After an hour, add the tamari, sugar, mirin, and dashi. Continue to cook on a low heat until the moisture has boiled away almost entirely and it is like a thick relish. Allow to cool. Sometimes I like to puree it for variation.

3 This can be served simply with rice. This relish will keep for two weeks in the fridge.

CLEAR BROTH WITH KIMCHI

If you're really stuck for time and know that the easy fast food option won't serve you well, then let me change your life with the quickest, most complex soup you have yet to taste.

One of the greatest pieces of advice I ever got was to always have a slow cooker on the go, doing something (this is mostly applicable in the winter, of course). In my case, this is generally some kind of stock or broth. After arriving home late one evening, I could smell the broth as it gently infused the kitchen. I was so hungry, and there was a jar of kimchi next to the slow cooker. It would not have been beyond me to have just tucked into the jar, but I craved something warm and nourishing. Without really realizing what I was doing, I was ladling broth into a bowl and adding a generous serving of kimchi. What could go wrong? Broth is good and kimchi is good, so I figured there was a fair chance that the two together would be good.

It was more than good. It was amazing, and the perfect example of fast slow food. To me, it doesn't get any better. **MAKES 1 BOWL**

I ladle of chicken or vegetable broth (or the quick Asian broth overleaf works well too)

I generous tablespoon kimchi

Simply ladle the warm broth into a bowl and add the kimchi. Eat and repeat.

QUICK ASIAN BROTH

This broth combines some of my favorite flavors. It could stand on its own as a savory drink or you could use it as the base for a light bowl of noodles, steamed greens and julienned vegetables, or your favorite protein.

MAKES 3 CUPS

3 stalks of lemongrass, topped, tailed, and crushed

2 to 3 red chilies, deseeded and sliced

3 garlic cloves, crushed

Thumb-sized piece of fresh ginger, peeled and sliced

Fingernail-sized piece of fresh turmeric, peeled and sliced

4 kaffir lime leaves

4 cups filtered water

Juice of 2 lemons or limes

Sea salt

Add the lemongrass, chilies, garlic, ginger, turmeric, and kaffir lime leaves to a pot and pour in the water. Bring to a boil over a medium-high heat, then lower to a simmer and cook for ten minutes. Remove from the heat and add the lemon juice and salt to taste. Cover and let the broth infuse for 30 minutes. Strain, discarding the solids, then reheat and use as needed.

BEET KVASS AND SAUERKRAUT SUMMER SOUP

For a more complex soup, this is a wonderful summer treat. It's easy to assemble from just a few components and it's best served cold so that you can really enjoy the complexity of the flavors. This recipe is influenced by a similar one in the Bar Tartine cookbook. **SERVES 4**

4 medium beets

3 tablespoons extra virgin olive oil

1 onion, diced

1 sweet potato or regular potato, peeled and chopped

2 cups dashi (page 180)

2 sprigs of fresh tarragon

1 teaspoon caraway seeds

1 pound sauerkraut (an herby kraut, dill and garlic kraut, or a caraway kraut would be particularly good)

3 cups beet kvass and the spent pickled beets (page 297)

6 to 7 fermented garlic cloves (page 68)

1 tablespoon raw honey

Sea salt and freshly ground black pepper

Yogurt, to serve

Fresh dill, to garnish

1 Preheat the oven to 350°F.

2 Wash the beets well and place them on a baking tray. Drizzle them lightly with a tablespoon of the olive oil and roast in the oven for about 45 minutes, until soft.

3 Meanwhile, place the onion, sweet potato, and dashi in a saucepan. Bring to a boil, then reduce the heat to a simmer and cook until the potato is soft. This makes a wonderful base for the soup. Remove from the heat, then add the tarragon and caraway seeds to infuse the soup as it cools.

4 Place the sauerkraut, kvass, beets (both roasted and pickled), garlic, honey, the remaining two tablespoons of olive oil, and the cooled dashi stock base in a high-speed blender and blend until smooth. You may need to do this in batches. Season to taste with salt and pepper, then refrigerate until ready to serve. Ladle into bowls and serve with a dollop of yogurt and garnish with fresh dill.

52 GARLIC CLOVE SOUP

When I first encountered this soup it sounded like a lot of garlic, but you'll be surprised—it's mellow, full of flavor, and will cure any suggestion of a cold or flu. Once you start peeling those little gems, it won't seem so daunting after all.

MAKES 1 QUART

26 garlic cloves, unpeeled (about 2 large bulbs)

2 tablespoons olive oil

Sea salt and freshly ground black pepper

2 tablespoons butter or coconut oil

I large onion, sliced

I ounce fresh ginger, peeled and minced

I¹/₂ teaspoons chopped fresh thyme

I heaped teaspoon ground turmeric

¹/₂ teaspoon cayenne pepper

3¹/₂ cups organic vegetable broth or chicken stock

26 fermented garlic cloves (page 68)

¹/₂ cup almond or coconut milk (homemade is best)

Lemon wedges, to serve

1 Preheat the oven to 340°F.

2 Place the 26 raw garlic cloves in a small glass baking dish. Drizzle with olive oil, sprinkle with sea salt, and toss to coat. Roast in the oven for about 45 minutes.

3 Melt the butter or coconut oil in a large saucepan set over a medium heat. Add the onion, ginger, thyme, turmeric, and cayenne and cook for about six minutes, until the onions are translucent. Squeeze the roasted garlic between your fingertips into the pan to release the cloves. Cook for a few minutes for the flavor to integrate. Add your broth, cover the pot with a lid, and simmer, covered, for about 20 minutes, until the garlic is very tender. Add the 26 fermented garlic cloves.

4 Puree the soup with an immersion blender or in a regular blender until smooth. Gradually add the milk, blending as you go. Season to taste. Pour back into the pot to reheat if necessary.

5 Serve in a warmed bowl with a squeeze of lemon and never fear the common cold again.

INDIAN BUTTERMILK SOUP

There isn't too much middle ground with buttermilk—you generally either love it or hate it. This soup, traditionally served cold, adds layers of sweet and spice to the zing of the buttermilk. **SERVES 4**

I teaspoon vegetable oil

$^1/_2$ onion, finely chopped

$^1/_2$ chili, deseeded and finely chopped

I large garlic clove, minced

I teaspoon ground coriander

$^1/_2$ teaspoon ground cumin

$^1/_8$ teaspoon ground turmeric

4 ears of fresh sweet corn, kernels cut off

3 cups buttermilk

$^3/_4$ teaspoon coarse salt

1 Heat the oil in a medium saucepan set over a medium heat. Add the onion, chili, and garlic. Sauté for about five minutes, until the onion is soft and translucent and the chili and garlic are tender and fragrant. Add the coriander, cumin, and turmeric and cook for about two minutes, until the spices are toasted and fragrant. Add the corn kernels and sauté for two to three minutes, until the corn is lightly browned. Remove from the heat and allow to cool.

2 Transfer about $1^3/_4$ cups of the corn mixture to a blender with the buttermilk and salt. Puree until smooth, then transfer to a large bowl or plastic storage container and stir in the remaining corn mixture. Cover and place in the fridge to chill for at least two or three hours. Remove from the fridge, ladle into bowls, and dig in.

SUPER GREEN SOUP WITH SAUERKRAUT

A high-powered blender such as a Vitamix will blend all the ingredients into a smooth, drinkable soup. If you don't have a high-powered blender, you can make this soup in smaller batches in a food processor. It will be chunkier but just as delicious. **SERVES 4**

³/₄ cup sauerkraut

2 celery stalks

I large or 2 small carrots

I ounce kale and/or spinach

¹/₂ cucumber

¹/₂ lemon, peeled

I garlic clove

5 sprigs of fresh cilantro

5 sprigs of fresh parsley

2¹/₂ cups filtered water

¹/₂ tablespoon olive oil

¹/₂ teaspoon sea alt

OPTIONAL TOPPINGS:

Chopped avocado

Crushed crackers

Chopped olives

Chopped cucumber

Chopped spring onion

Chopped peppers

Activated nuts and seeds

Herby sauerkraut

Fresh herbs

1 Roughly chop all the soup ingredients and place in a Vitamix or other high-powered blender. Blend for one minute.

2 Serve the soup cold in bowls with your favorite toppings from the list. If you like a little warmth, you can gently heat this soup to 100°F without destroying the probiotic benefits.

CREAMY CUCUMBER SOUP

Soups largely feature as warming bowls for autumn and winter months, but I have fallen for cold soups as a wonderful quick summer fix. It feels like it has taken me a few years to appreciate cold soups (spending time in hotter climates helps!), but they're a quick and easy way to incorporate any leftover brines from fermenting. **SERVES 1**

I cucumber, chopped

I avocado, stoned, halved, and flesh scooped out

$^1/_2$ medium onion, chopped

I fermented garlic clove (page 68)

$^1/_2$ cup leftover brine (dilly bean brine works best—see page 52)

$^1/_2$ cup filtered water

2 tablespoons olive oil

Sea salt and freshly ground black pepper

Chopped fresh dill, to garnish

This couldn't be easier—simply blend it all up. Season to taste and serve cold with chopped fresh dill. The flavors are fresh and vibrant, but if you like a little warmth, you can gently heat this soup to 100°F without destroying the probiotic benefits.

HEALING BOWL

A quick, hearty bowl of comforting soup. **SERVES 4**

2 cups chicken or vegetable stock

2¹/₂ to 3¹/₂ cups cooked butter beans

¹/₃ cup cooked rice (preferably brown rice)

I egg, beaten

2 large bunches of spinach, chopped

2 bunches of fresh cilantro, chopped, plus extra to garnish

I large bunch of fresh parsley, chopped

I large bunch of fresh dill, chopped

Handful of fresh mint leaves, chopped, plus extra to garnish

Handful of fresh basil leaves, chopped, plus extra to garnish

4 cups milk kefir (page 134)

2 cups yogurt

I teaspoon raw apple cider vinegar or kombucha vinegar (page 318)

Sea salt, to taste

2 spring onions, finely chopped, to garnish

1 Place your stock in a saucepan with the cooked butter beans, rice, and beaten egg and whisk everything together. Cook on a medium heat, stirring frequently, for ten minutes. Add the spinach and herbs and simmer for another ten minutes, continuing to stir. Remove from the heat and add the kefir and yogurt, stirring it through. Finally, add the vinegar, then season to taste with salt.

2 Serve immediately or cool to room temperature and then transfer to the fridge. Garnish with the cilantro, mint, and basil leaves, and the chopped spring onions.

THE FERMENTED FIX:

SNACKS, STARTERS,

AND SUPER-FAST

SUPERFOOD

SINCE I STARTED FERMENTING, creating meals has dramatically changed the way we eat and operate in the kitchen. Gone are the days when sauces were cooked up from a base of onion and garlic and I can't remember when I last made something as laborious as lasagne.

Nowadays, there is a lot of whizzing and whirring in a blender as ingredients are piled in to make a raw sauce, soup, pâté, or paste, and it only takes seconds. There is usually one pan or pot on the hob containing the protein element, there is usually some kind of salad, and then there are jars and jars of different things to choose from to make the plate jump with joy.

A huge bonus of having a range of fermented foods on the go is that you can have fast slow food for lunch or dinner. The recipes in this section are ideas for incorporating ferments into your diet as snacks, entrées, lunches, dinners, and more. They are also wonderful as sharing plates for a dinner party to show your guests that fermentation creates fun, funky food that's full of flavor. They work because you have jars of goodness already made and in your fridge, waiting for the right moment to appear on your plate.

VEGGIE STICKS WITH MISO AND WALNUT DIP

*I like to use activated nuts, which are simply nuts that I have soaked and then dehydrated to bring out their crispy, crunchy texture. If you don't have a dehydrator, you can toast the nuts in the oven first to release the flavor and break down the phytic acid, which is the method that this recipe uses. Or you can skip this step entirely and just use four tablespoons of a good-quality shop-bought nut butter. **MAKES 1 X ½-PINT JAR OF MISO DIP***

3 tablespoons blanched almonds

3 tablespoons walnuts

¼ cup miso

3 tablespoons warm filtered water

Squeeze of lime juice

1 to 2 teaspoons mirin (optional)

1 jar of fermented carrot sticks (page 58), to serve

1 Preheat the oven to 350°F.

2 Spread the nuts in a pie plate and toast in the oven for eight minutes. Allow to cool, then grind in a mini food processor to a paste.

3 In a medium bowl, mix the nut paste and miso with the water and lime juice to form a dip. If you'd like some extra sweetness, add the mirin.

4 Serve with the fermented carrot sticks for dipping. The miso dip will keep in the fridge for three days.

Incorporating fermented foods onto the modern-day abundance plate

Are you wondering how to eat your cultured veggies in a gluten-free, sugar-free, mostly dairy-free, whole foods kind of way? It's a common question, so here are a few simple ways to get started.

- Add them to stir-fries, curries, or vegetable sauces at the end of cooking.

- Blend into a soup at the end of cooking.

- For a quick meal or appetizer, smother flatbread or flaxseed crackers with fermented bean dip, nut cheese, fermented pesto, or tapenade and top with a spoonful of kraut or cultured veggies. Throw a pickle on the side.

- Add some fermented salsa, relish, or chutney to a salad bowl or add to green, bean, grain, or meat salads.

- Puree into a quick sauce or dressing for salads, steamed vegetables, or grains.

- Use as a vegetable side dish for your protein dishes.

- Add to collard wraps or tortillas. Cultured vegetables and beans or rice take Mexican food to another level.

- Add to sushi rolls.

- Or eat as is, straight from the jar—just use a clean fork each time!

The Cultured Club open sandwich challenge

Many conversations with my friends have started with the questions, "Why ferment? Why veer so far away from common foods, like the sandwich, for example?"

There was a time when a sandwich was a part of my lunch every day. In fact, during one project I was working on, there was a café nearby that prided itself on serving the biggest, fullest sandwiches around. Half the sandwich would usually be reserved for dinner and the digestion process took hours out of the day. For me, "why ferment?" has a lot to do with digestion. If I can get the same energy from food but have less digestive work to do, I'm happy.

So I set myself a challenge: Could a sandwich be made in such a way that it would be easier to digest? The answer is yes!

Loosely inspired by the creative offerings of the Danish smørrebrød, here's what you need for a simple open sandwich:

- I slice of bread (see the breads on pages 154–158)
- Cultured butter—keep it plain or go for a fun flavor (page 143)
- Fermented mustard (pages 112–113)
- Lacto-fermented mayonnaise (page 115)
- Soft cheese, like gouda
- Cucumber pickles (page 77)

Simply layer it all up and enjoy it one easy mouthful at a time.

GRAB 'N' GO FOCACCIA

Once you have integrated fermented foods into your kitchen, there will be a shift in your routine. When you have established a good collection of fermented goods in your pantry, you'll no longer spend hours at the stove. Meals can become a spontaneous grab-and-go affair, knowing that you have offered up something wonderfully nutritious. **SERVES 1**

I slice of flaxseed focaccia (page 157)
....
$^{1}/_{2}$ avocado, sliced
....
I teaspoon lemon juice
....
I to 2 tablespoons sauerkraut
....
A splash of olive oil
....
Microgreens, to garnish

Simply assemble as for any open-face sandwich: lay the avocado slices on the bread and drizzle with the lemon juice. (Feel free to swap out the avocado for nut cheese or some hummus.) Top with a generous serving of kraut and a drizzle of olive oil, then garnish with microgreens.

FERMENTED CRACKERS WITH LABNEH AND SAUERKRAUT

My favorite go-to snack! I love everything about this combination of tastes, textures, and all-round deliciousness. I could easily eat this and only this. If you have these ingredients sitting in your fridge, they're just waiting to be put together for your quickest superfood snack. My favorite topping is avocado and gobs of The Cultured Club's fermented tomato salsa (page 82). Or break loose and combine whatever dips, spreads, and relishes you have. To boost this combination into a fulfilling and nourishing lunch or light dinner, turn it into a salad bowl with sauerkraut, nut cheese, relish, and fermented crackers.

SERVES 1

Baby salad leaves

I serving of sauerkraut (plain, dill and garlic, or caraway work well)

Nut cheese (pages 148–149) or labneh cheese (page 138)

Apple relish (page 99)

Thinly sliced radishes or ribbons of kohlrabi or celeriac

Fermented flaxseed and onion crackers (page 160)

Your favorite oil

I avocado, stoned, halved, and sliced

Simply layer up the salad leaves, sauerkraut, nut cheese, relish, and veggies on your crackers. Drizzle with your favorite oil and top with sliced avocado.

PORTOBELLO MUSHROOMS WITH LABNEH AND PISTACHIO PESTO

The mushroom will combine well with lots of different flavors, be it fruity, herby, nutty, or meaty. There are so many options, but this one is a wonderful start. This will make a great snack or it can take center stage on the plate of a more satisfying main meal. **MAKES 4 MUSHROOMS**

4 portobello mushrooms
3 tablespoons tamari
2 teaspoons lime juice
$1/2$ teaspoon olive oil
4 tablespoons kefir pistachio pesto (page 127)
4 tablespoons labneh cheese (page 138)
Fresh chopped herbs or watercress, to garnish

1 Preheat the grill to full heat.

2 Remove the brown gills from the underside of the mushroom caps using a spoon and remove the stems. (Don't throw out the gills and stems—they can be saved for the kitchen scraps vegetable stock on page 179.)

3 Combine the tamari, lime juice, and olive oil in a small bowl, then brush this over both sides of the mushroom caps. Place the mushroom caps on the grill rack, stem sides down, and grill for five minutes on each side, until soft.

4 To serve, fill each mushroom with a tablespoon of pesto, then add a tablespoon of labneh cheese on top. Garnish with fresh herbs or watercress.

SUPER QUICK SAUERKRAUT SEED BOWL

Consider this an upgrade to first class from just eating sauerkraut straight from the jar, economy style. **SERVES 1**

I cup raw sauerkraut

$^1/_2$ to I avocado, stoned, halved, and sliced

2 tablespoons mix of pumpkin, sunflower, sesame, hemp seeds, and/or golden flaxseeds, toasted

I tablespoon nutritional yeast (optional)

$^1/_4$ teaspoon onion powder

$^1/_4$ teaspoon ground cumin

Pinch of sea salt (optional, depending on how salty you made the sauerkraut)

Combine everything in a bowl and eat with your fingers if you like.

RICE BOWL WITH FURIKAKE, SEAWEED RELISH, AND SPICY SEAWEED KRAUT

My kids and husband like rice, so I often have a surplus of it. Using leftover rice is no concern as long as it has not been left sitting around at room temperature. You can safely keep rice in the fridge, stored in an airtight container, for up to four days, which is plenty of time to use it up, especially in this quick and easy rice bowl. **SERVES 2**

2 to 4 tablespoons furikake seasoning (page III)

2 cups cooked rice

4 tablespoons super spicy seaweed kraut (page 38)

2 tablespoons seaweed relish (page 181)

2 teaspoons tamari or liquid aminos (optional)

Mix the furikake seasoning through the rice, then divide the rice between two bowls. Top with seaweed kraut and seaweed relish. Season with tamari if necessary, but it should already be a very flavorful bowl.

Eggs

For the little bit of animal protein that features in my diet, eggs are a favorite. The debate continues to evolve as to whether or not they are good or bad, but for me, the story of food is at the forefront of the argument. Making sure you buy the highest-quality eggs possible is a powerful consumer message that may someday inspire change. It's organic, free-range eggs only for me.

FERMENTED EGGS

Does the idea of fermented eggs strike fear into your heart as you envisage a jar full of a noxious sulfuric odor? Unless you try this, you will never know the joys of a firm and already salted egg, which bears no resemblance to the more common pickled egg. **MAKES 1 X 1-QUART JAR**

8 organic, free-range eggs (enough to fill a 1-quart jar)

2 to 2¹/₂ cups filtered water (enough to cover the eggs)

4 tablespoons starter, such as leftover brine from a previous ferment

1 tablespoon sea salt

1 Place your eggs in a saucepan and completely submerge them in cold water. Include a few inches of extra water. Turn the heat to high and wait for the water to boil. As soon as it does, cover the pot with a tightly fitting lid, turn off the heat, and set a timer for ten minutes. After the ten minutes are up, remove them from the pan with a slotted spoon and cool them off immediately by placing them in very cold water. The cold water bath not only makes them easier to peel, but it also stops the cooking and will prevent a gray ring from appearing around the yolk. Peel the eggs and leave whole.

2 Place the peeled eggs in a clean wide-mouthed 1-quart jar and pour in the filtered water, starter, and salt, adding enough water to completely submerge the eggs in the liquid but still making sure you leave 1 inch of headspace at the top of the jar.

3 Allow the eggs to soak for between three and seven days at room temperature. Store them in the fridge in the jar you fermented them in and remove them as you'd like to eat them, keeping in mind that they will get more acidic and colorful as time progresses. They will keep well for two to three weeks.

MISO MARINATED EGGS (MISO TAMAGO)

I like to do batches of six at a time. One day you will want to make it with your own homemade miso!

PER EGG

1 organic, free-range egg

2 tablespoons white miso of your choice (homemade one day!)

1 teaspoon maple syrup

1 Place your chosen number of eggs into a saucepan and completely submerge them in cold water. Include a few inches of extra water. Turn the heat to high and wait for the water to boil. As soon as it does, cover the pot with a tightly fitting lid, turn off the heat, and set a timer for ten minutes. After the ten minutes are up, remove them from the pan with a slotted spoon and cool them off immediately by placing them in very cold water. The cold water bath not only makes them easier to peel, but it also stops the cooking and will prevent a gray ring from appearing around the yolk. Peel the eggs and leave whole.

2 Mix the miso and maple syrup together very well to form a smooth paste. Spread the paste over the middle of a piece of plastic wrap or a ziplock bag that's big enough to wrap the egg in. Put one egg in the middle of the plastic wrap and wrap it around the egg. Twist the plastic shut at the top and squeeze until the miso is completely covering the egg. Place in the fridge for at least five hours but up to one week.

3 When you're ready to use an egg, take off the plastic wrap. The white of the egg should be a light to medium beige and the surface will be covered with a bit of miso. You can leave this on or wipe it off gently if you prefer.

BEET KVASS EGGS

If anything these are worth doing just once, as they are super impressive and really tasty. Once is all it takes to fall in love with them. These eggs are outrageously fun and a real talking point. Throw a dinner party just so you can make these. **MAKES 1 X 1-QUART JAR**

6 to 8 organic, free-range eggs

3 thin slices of raw onion

$^1/_2$ tablespoon allspice berries

3 cups beet kvass (page 297)

1 Place your eggs in a saucepan and completely submerge them in cold water. Include a few inches of extra water. Turn the heat to high and wait for the water to boil. As soon as it does, cover the pot with a tightly fitting lid, turn off the heat, and set a timer for ten minutes. After the ten minutes are up, remove them from the pan with a slotted spoon and cool them off immediately by placing them in very cold water. The cold water bath not only makes them easier to peel, but it also stops the cooking and will prevent a gray ring from appearing around the yolk. Peel the eggs and leave whole.

2 Place the onion slices and allspice berries in the bottom of a clean wide-mouthed 1-quart jar.

3 Place the peeled eggs in the jar, then pour in enough beet kvass to cover the eggs, making sure you leave 1 inch of headspace at the top of the jar. Secure the jar with a lid.

4 Place in the refrigerator for three to four days before eating, then keep refrigerated and eat within a week.

MISO MARINTAED EGGS

BEET KVASS EGGS

KOMBUCHA MUSTARD

BEET KVASS EGGS WITH FERMENTED MAYONNAISE AND DUKKAH

Fermented beets make a wonderful drink called beet kvass (page 297), which is used here to preserve eggs for a lengthy period of time. **SERVES 2**

4 tablespoons lacto-fermented mayonnaise (page 115)

4 beet kvass eggs (page 211)

Pinch of dukkah (page 110)

1 Make a generous circle of fermented mayonnaise on your plate. Take a beet kvass egg from the jar, allowing the liquid to drip away, then place in the middle of the mayonnaise and sprinkle with dukkah.

2 To boost this starter to a lunch dish, serve it as a salad with some romaine lettuce, beet tapenade (page 123), or green olive and preserved lemon tapenade (page 122) and fermented flaxseed and onion crackers (page 160).

RAMEN EGGS

Not technically a ferment, but still incredibly delicious and a little less messy than the miso marinated eggs recipe on page 210. **MAKES 2 EGGS**

2 organic, free-range eggs

2 tablespoons soy sauce or tamari

2 tablespoons mirin

6 tablespoons filtered water

1 You want these eggs to be soft-boiled. The best way to do this is to bring a pan of water to a boil, then reduce to a simmer and place the eggs in for seven minutes. After the seven minutes are up, remove them from the pan with a slotted spoon and cool them off immediately by placing them in very cold water. The cold water bath not only makes them easier to peel, but it also stops the cooking. Once they are cooled, peel the eggs and leave them whole. As they are soft-boiled, they are not completely hardened, so be gentle as you peel them.

2 Combine the soy sauce, mirin, and water in a small jar or ziplock bag. Pop the peeled eggs into the marinade and leave overnight in the fridge to flavor them. Eat within two days.

EGGS ANY WAY WITH TONS OF KIMCHI OVER SALAD

When kimchi first entered my life, I had it for lunch pretty much every day. I would quickly toss together some salad leaves (spinach, arugula, or lamb's lettuce), wild flowers, pea shoots, sprouts, and some grated carrots and radish if I was lucky, and a generous serving of kimchi. This would be topped with eggs—poached, fried, scrambled, soft-boiled, or omelets all go well with kimchi (or you can easily substitute the eggs with tofu if you're vegan). It was a tasty lunch that not only satisfied me, but my husband too. To make this into a more substantial meal, serve with noodles or some soaked oats bread (page 154) or vegetable bread slices (page 158) or some sliced avocado or roasted sweet potato fries. This is super nutritious slow food, ready in a flash. All the hard work has been done by your kimchi as it sits on a shelf and subtly ferments away. SERVES 2

1 bag of salad leaves
6 fresh radishes, thinly sliced
2 carrots, grated or julienned
1 tablespoon avocado or another mild oil
4 to 6 tablespoons kimchi
2 organic, free-range eggs, cooked as desired
Sprouts, pea shoots, or microgreens, to garnish

1 Fill a bowl with the salad leaves, toss with the radishes and carrots, and dress with a splash of oil.

2 Divide the salad between two bowls and top with a generous serving of kimchi and an egg. Garnish with sprouts, pea shoots, or microgreens and serve.

Pickled plates

Enjoying fermented foods at every meal is a great way to ensure digestive ease and to create a healthy ecosystem of bacteria in the digestive tract. Eating just sauerkraut at every meal isn't particularly appetizing, though, so having a wide selection of ferments on hand will allow for lots of variety. For example, a stir-fry is made all the more vibrant with a serving of kimchi and classic meals can always find a fermented twist.

So grab some fermented veggie sticks and whiz up some miso and walnut dip while I share a selection of meals with a probiotic twist.

CABBAGE ROLLS WITH VEGETABLES AND MUSHROOMS

Cabbage rolls are a dish associated with Eastern Europe. They are a Christmas tradition called sarma, originating in Romania: sour cabbage is stuffed and cooked with a pork and beef mix. These little parcels have been given a new place on the table. They are an unbelievable taste sensation.

MAKES 10 ROLLS

I cup raw walnuts

2 tablespoons coconut oil

I bunch of spring onions, sliced

I red pepper, deseeded and cut into small dice

6 fermented mushrooms (page 86)

I fermented garlic clove (page 68)

4 tablespoons nutritional yeast

I teaspoon ground cumin

I teaspoon chili powder

Sea salt

I cup fresh corn kernels

$^1/_2$ jalapeño pepper, deseeded and finely chopped

2 tablespoons finely chopped fresh cilantro

10 cabbage leaves

1 Activate the walnuts by soaking them overnight.

2 Heat the oil in a pan set over a medium heat, then add the spring onions and red pepper and sauté for ten minutes, until soft. Transfer to a food processor with the walnuts, mushrooms, garlic, nutritional yeast, cumin, chili powder, and a pinch of sea salt and briefly pulse, leaving it quite coarse. Transfer to a bowl and stir in the corn, jalapeño, and cilantro.

3 Taking one cabbage leaf at a time, place two tablespoons of the filling on each leaf. Start at the bottom, where the stem begins, and roll upwards, following the stem. Once you have rolled to the halfway point, fold in the sides. Continue rolling until it's completely closed.

4 Place the stuffed cabbage rolls in the dehydrator and dehydrate for four to six hours at 110°F if desired for a drier, crispier cabbage roll.

ZUCCHINI WRAPS WITH LEMON LABNEH CHEESE, POMEGRANATE SEEDS, AND NASTURTIUM CAPERS

Not only are these delicious little bite-sized appetizers, but they are rather impressive-looking little creations too. **SERVES 4**

I zucchini, peeled into thin strips to make 4 substantial "wraps"

4 tablespoons lemon labneh cheese (page 138)

4 teaspoons raw honey

4 teaspoons pomegranate seeds

4 teaspoons nasturtium capers (page 55), to garnish (optional)

Place one tablespoon of the cheese on a zucchini slice. Roll up and add a tiny dot of cheese at the end to stick the roll together so that it holds its shape. Stand upright on the plate and top with the honey, pomegranate seeds, and nasturtium capers, if using.

KEFIR MACKEREL PÂTÉ

I often make a batch of mackerel pâté when I have an abundance of labneh. It's a handy way to introduce some fermented foods by stealth to the uninitiated. After all, there are times when less is more! **MAKES 1 X 1-PINT JAR**

3 freshly cooked or smoked mackerel fillets

I cup labneh cheese (page 138)

I cup cultured cream (page 142) (or more kefir cheese)

3 teaspoons fermented horseradish (page 64) (optional)

I lemon, zest of whole lemon and juice of $^1/_2$

Small handful of fresh dill, finely chopped

Freshly ground black pepper

1 Skin the mackerel fillets and remove any bones, then flake the mackerel into the bowl of a food processor. Add the kefir cheese, kefir cream, horseradish relish (if using), and lemon zest and whiz until smooth. Add lemon juice to taste, then fold through the dill and a good grinding of black pepper.

2 Spoon into a clean pint jar and store in the fridge for up to one month.

COLLARD WRAPS WITH KEFIR MACKEREL PÂTÉ, RADISHES, AND CUCUMBER PICKLES

Eating more greens just feels good, so I choose to whenever I can over the convenience of a slice of bread spread with pâté. Collard leaves are a great option, as they're flexible, strong and tasty, and will neatly hold all that delicious goodness together for you. **SERVES 1**

I collard leaf

2 tablespoons kefir mackerel pâté (page 220)

I large radish, thinly sliced

I tablespoon sliced cucumber pickle (page 77)

Fresh dill sprigs, to garnish

1 Trim the stem from the collard leaf. You can soften the leaf by giving it a quick blanch in some hot water and then transferring it to an ice bath to cool.

2 Assemble your wrap by smearing the leaf with the kefir mackerel pâté. Top with some sliced radishes and some cucumber pickle. Garnish with dill, then roll up tightly and serve.

DOSAS WITH SPICY POTATO FILLING

There are hardly any countries in the world that don't have some version of the humble pancake—they are practically as old as civilization itself. From okonomiyaki, as they are known in Japan, to crêpes in France, with a selection of dosas, appams, idlis, tortillas, and injeras along the way, pancakes can make for quite an interesting study on cultural variations. I'm guessing that their creation was a practical solution to the absence of cutlery, a way to scoop up food without too much mess. The dosa is a thin savory pancake made by fermenting rice and lentils. It's served with a host of flavorful accompaniments, such as spiced potatoes and chutneys. **SERVES 4**

I cup red quinoa or rice

³/₄ cup red lentils

I tablespoon fenugreek (optional, but it adds a nice flavor)

¹/₂ teaspoon sea salt

2 cups filtered water

Oil, for cooking

FOR THE SPICY POTATO FILLING:

About I²/₃ pounds potatoes, peeled and chopped into small cubes

3 tablespoons coconut oil

2 teaspoons black mustard seeds

2 teaspoons cumin seeds

2 teaspoons fennel seeds

Thumb-sized piece of fresh ginger, peeled and finely chopped

I large onion, halved and thinly sliced

2 garlic cloves, crushed

4 fresh or dried curry leaves

I teaspoon ground turmeric

I teaspoon ground coriander

¹/₄ teaspoon chili powder

TO SERVE:

I small bunch of fresh cilantro, finely chopped

Coconut chutney (page 107)

Happy fermented chili sauce (page 118)

1 To make the dosas, place the quinoa, lentils, fenugreek, and salt in a bowl and cover with cold water. Allow to sit for four to six hours or overnight if you prefer.

2 Drain and rinse, then pop into a blender. Add the filtered water and blend until smooth. Pour the batter into a bowl and set on the counter, uncovered, for one to two days. You'll see bubbles forming and the batter will puff up as the fermentation progresses. The scent will gradually become more and more sour.

3 Prior to cooking, stir the batter with a spoon until it's smooth and the texture of runny cream. Heat a pan over a medium heat and grease with a little oil.

4 Pour $^3/_4$ cup of batter into the pan, tilting the pan in a circle to spread the batter more widely and evenly. In southern India, a ladle is traditionally used to spread the batter thinly in the pan and cook it as a crispy crêpe, which makes it easier to place a filling inside and use as a wrap. Although not necessary, I like to place a lid over the pan as the dosa cooks, as it seems to help the topside cook through more completely and quickly. Once the top of the dosa is no longer the consistency of batter and it looks cooked through, flip it over and cook for another one to two minutes. Repeat with the remaining batter, or any unused batter will last another couple of days in the refrigerator. Just stir the batter each time before using, until creamy and smooth.

5 To make the filling, bring a pan of water to a boil, then add the potatoes, reduce the heat, and simmer for ten to 15 minutes, until soft. Drain the potatoes and set aside.

6 Melt the coconut oil in a pan set over a low heat, then add the mustard seeds. Once they start to pop, add the cumin and fennel seeds and the chopped ginger and cook for 30 seconds, then add the onions and garlic and cook just until the onions turn translucent. Add the curry leaves, turmeric, ground coriander, and chili powder, then add the potatoes to the party, stirring them into the onion and spice mix to disperse the flavor.

7 Spoon some of the filling into the dosas. Garnish with the chopped fresh cilantro and serve with coconut chutney and fermented chili sauce for some extra heat.

BUCKWHEAT AND MILLET SUPERFOOD KIMCHI PANCAKES

The traditional idea of a pancake has been blown wide open for me after a week of whipping up various combinations on a BBQ plate, of all places. The new discoveries are liberating. This will not fail to capture your imagination.

MAKES 4 PANCAKES

$^1/_2$ pound buckwheat groats
I cup millet
2 tablespoons acidic medium such as whey, lemon juice, or raw apple cider vinegar
I cup kimchi
4 teaspoons coconut oil
Yangnyeomjang dipping sauce (page III), to serve

1 Place the buckwheat and millet in a medium bowl. Add $1^2/_3$ cups of filtered water and the acidic medium and soak overnight.

2 The following day, drain and rinse the grains. Pop them into your blender and add an equal amount of filtered water (about 2 cups). Blend until you have a smooth pancake batter, then stir in the kimchi, mixing it in thoroughly.

3 Heat one teaspoon of coconut oil in a frying pan set over a medium heat. Pour in a quarter of the batter and let the pancake cook for three to five minutes. It's ready to flip when bubbles form on the top and the batter becomes almost opaque. Cook on the other side until golden brown, then transfer to a plate and keep warm. Repeat until all your batter is used up, adding one teaspoon of coconut oil to the pan each time.

4 Serve with the dipping sauce. Store any leftovers in the fridge for up to three days.

Sauerkraut pancakes

While kimchi pancakes have their origins deeply cemented in Korean culture, why not try a sauerkraut pancake? It's guaranteed to be just as satisfying.

I know that cooking the kraut won't be so kind on all those little microbes you have cultivated, so before you lose faith in me, I suggest that you choose whatever sauerkraut you have and pair it with some other fermented delight in your fridge. It will be hard to go wrong and it might even be a wonderful service to the dregs of a jar that has otherwise lost its charm. Simply make the pancake batter as for the kimchi pancakes on the previous page, swapping sauerkraut for the kimchi.

Here are some delicious variations to get you started:

- Beet and kohlrabi veggie surprise sauerkraut (page 33) with fig and olive tapenade (page 122)

- Apple ginger kraut (page 33) with mango chutney (page 107)

- Golden kraut (page 33) with apple five-spice relish (page 99)

- Hola curtido kraut (page 33) with chili sauce (page 118)

- Super hulk kraut (page 36) with tomato salsa (page 82)

- Krishna kraut (page 39) with raisin and spice relish (page 106) or mango chutney (page 107)

- Or just simply reach for the fermented mayonnaise (page 115), mustard (pages 112–113), or ketchup (page 117) and smear it on your pancake.

INDIAN SOCCA WITH CASHEW NUT CHEESE AND SWEET AND SPICY ONION RELISH

Life can be very dull when gluten leaves the party until you find something that takes its place. While these socca are perfect for dipping into curries and stews, they make a fine dish on their own with generous helpings of fermented goodness. **MAKES 4 PANCAKES**

I¹/₂ cups chickpea flour

I teaspoon sea salt

¹/₂ teaspoon ground coriander

¹/₂ teaspoon ground ginger

¹/₂ teaspoon ground turmeric

¹/₂ teaspoon curry powder

¹/₂ teaspoon nigella seeds

¹/₄ teaspoon cayenne pepper

¹/₄ teaspoon mustard powder

2 cups sparkling water

Coconut oil or ghee, for frying

TO SERVE:

Grated carrots

Sweet and spicy onion relish (page 71)

Hard cheese (page 149—use cashews instead of almonds)

Microgreens, to garnish

1 Place the chickpea flour, salt, and spices in a large bowl. Gradually pour in the sparkling water, stirring as you go to create a smooth batter.

2 Heat the coconut oil or ghee in a pan set over a medium heat. Pour in ¹/₄ cup of the batter, allowing it to spread out evenly and thinly around the pan. When bubbles appear evenly over the surface, flip the socca over to cook on the other side. Slide the pancake out of the pan and repeat with the remaining batter.

3 To assemble, arrange a socca on a plate. Top with grated carrots and a little sweet and spicy onion relish and crumble the cashew nut cheese over the top. Garnish with microgreens and serve.

AVOCADO PESTO TARTS WITH A NUT CRUST

You can use six or seven tablespoons of any fermented pesto from your supply (see pages 127–128) or you can use the fresh pesto in this recipe, although it won't be fermented. Use activated nuts from your stash, meaning they have been soaked overnight and dehydrated (see page 165). If you don't have any activated nuts on hand, roast them in an oven preheated to 340°F for ten minutes, until golden, to help release the phytates.

MAKES 6 INDIVIDUAL TARTS

2¹/₂ ounces fresh basil

I handful of almonds

I small handful of sunflower seeds

I medium garlic clove, grated

4 to 5 tablespoons extra virgin olive oil

2 to 3 tablespoons lemon juice, plus extra if needed

Sea salt and freshly ground black pepper

I avocado, stoned, halved, and flesh scooped out

¹/₂ preserved lemon (page 97), finely chopped, to garnish

FOR THE CRUST:

³/₄ cup almonds

I small fermented garlic clove (page 68), grated

4 tablespoons extra virgin olive oil (I used cold-pressed), plus extra for brushing

4 tablespoons sesame seeds

4 tablespoons flaxseeds, ground

4 tablespoons sunflower seeds, crushed

2 tablespoons freshly squeezed lemon juice

Sea salt and freshly ground black pepper

1 Place all the crust ingredients in a food processor or blender and process until completely mixed. Divide the crust mixture in half, then divide each half into three equal parts. This will give you six equal parts. Press the mixture into a round tart shape or press into individual tart pans, brush with a little olive oil, and pop in the fridge.

2 Place the basil, almonds, sunflower seeds, garlic, oil, lemon juice, and seasoning in a food processor and whiz until nicely blended, then blend six or seven tablespoons of the pesto with the avocado. Taste and season with more salt, pepper, or lemon juice if needed. When you're happy with the taste, scoop the avocado pesto filling into the tart shapes and return to the fridge.

3 Serve cold with a salad and a side of steamed greens and garnish with some finely chopped preserved lemon.

Don't throw out your avocado stones!

The seed is actually the most nutrient-dense part of an avocado and it's completely edible. More than 65 percent of the amino acids can be found in the avocado seed. It also contains more fiber than many other foods.

Since avocado seeds are exceptionally bitter, it's best to pair them with strong flavors. It can be grated over your sandwich or salads, or if you have a high-speed blender, you can incorporate it into smoothies or shakes.

Simply take the stone from the avocado and cut it into quarters. The soft inner seed is much easier to work with and it can be grated or blended easily.

POLENTA WITH CARAMELIZED ONIONS AND FERMENTED MUSHROOMS

I have fallen for polenta, a powerhouse of nutrition like no other. It is commonly served as a creamy porridge, but I prefer to let it cool and set, allowing me to chop it into bite-sized nuggets. If you aren't ready to delve into a fermented mushroom accompaniment, try serving this with some tomatoes and the sweet and spicy onion relish on page 71. **SERVES 4**

FOR THE POLENTA:

½ cup polenta, plus a little extra for coating

¾ cup filtered water

2 cups vegetable stock (page 179)

1 tablespoon butter

¾ cup grated Parmesan cheese or 4 tablespoons nutritional yeast

1 teaspoon sea salt

2 tablespoons coconut oil

FOR THE CARAMELIZED ONIONS:

2 teaspoons ghee or coconut oil

2 large onions, chopped

1 tablespoon coconut sugar

1 tablespoon balsamic vinegar

TO SERVE:

Fermented mushrooms (page 86)

Chopped fresh herbs such as thyme or marjoram

1 First soak the polenta for a few hours in the ¾ cup of water before cooking it. This helps to fully hydrate the cornmeal and therefore reduce the cooking time.

2 When it's time to start cooking, drain the polenta. Bring the vegetable stock and butter to a boil in a medium saucepan. Reduce the heat to medium-low and gradually whisk in the polenta, stirring until it becomes thick and creamy. This may take up to ten minutes. Remove from the heat and stir in the Parmesan and salt. Grease a baking tray with one tablespoon of the coconut oil (I use a 8-by-12-inch tray) and pour the polenta into the prepared tray, leveling it with the back of a spoon, and leave to set.

3 To make the caramelized onions, melt the ghee or coconut oil in a large frying pan set over a medium-low heat, then add the onions. Reduce the heat to low and cook the onions for about ten minutes, until soft. Add the coconut sugar and balsamic vinegar and cook for a further ten minutes, until caramelized. Set aside in a bowl.

4 Cut the polenta into bite-sized squares and coat in uncooked polenta. Heat the remaining tablespoon of coconut oil in a large frying pan set over a medium heat, then add the polenta squares and fry for two to three minutes on each side, until golden. Drain on a plate lined with paper towels.

5 To serve, top the polenta squares with a small amount of caramelized onions and some fermented mushrooms, then garnish with chopped fresh herbs.

SWEET POTATO BOATS WITH AVOCADO BUTTER, HORSERADISH SOUR CREAM, GOMASIO, AND CHILI KALE CRISPS

This is a quick evening fix if your pantry is well established. Feel free to experiment—it is for the imagination. For a Mexican twist, substitute some of the bean paste on page 241 for the horseradish and pull out the tomato salsa on page 82 and the kefir sour cream on page 142. **SERVES 4**

4 medium sweet potatoes

Pinch of smoked paprika (optional)

Sea salt and freshly ground black pepper

Chili kale crisps (page 237), to serve

FOR THE AVOCADO BUTTER:

2 teaspoons cumin seeds

2 small ripe avocados, stoned, halved, and flesh scooped out

I garlic clove, minced

4 tablespoons cultured butter (page 143), at room temperature

I tablespoon chopped fresh cilantro

I tablespoon lemon juice

Kosher salt and freshly ground black pepper

FOR THE GOMASIO:

I tablespoon smoked sea salt

$^3/_4$ cup unhulled raw black sesame seeds

FOR THE HORSERADISH SOUR CREAM:

$^1/_2$ cup kefir sour cream (page 142)

I tablespoon grated fresh horseradish

1 To make the avocado butter, heat a dry frying pan over a medium heat, then add the cumin seeds. Toast for a few minutes, shaking the pan occasionally, until the seeds are fragrant. Place all the ingredients in the bowl of a food processor and blend until well combined. Spoon the mixture onto a sheet of parchment paper and shape into a log, then roll up and twist the ends of the paper. Refrigerate for three to four hours. Store for up to three days in the refrigerator or a week in the freezer (you can also slice it and serve with grilled fish, chicken, or corn on the cob).

2 To cook the sweet potatoes, preheat the oven to 400°F.

3 This is the lazy way to cook a sweet potato—just prick the sweet potatoes with a fork three or four times and place them directly on the oven rack. Place a sheet of foil over the bottom of the oven to catch any syrup from the sweet potatoes that might drip out as they cook. Bake for 45 minutes or up to one hour if they're large, until cooked through and tender. When they're done, turn off the oven but let them sit in the warm oven for at least 30 minutes. I tend to make good use of the cooking time and make extra, as these can be stored by removing the skin and popping them into a sealed container in the fridge for up to three days. For example, you could use one for the masala quinoa croquettes on page 242.

4 To make the gomasio, heat a medium-sized pan on medium-low heat. Add the salt and toast for three minutes, then remove the salt and add the sesame seeds, stirring frequently until fragrant. You will hear some popping. Be sure to keep the heat low enough to avoid any burning. If you do burn them, throw them out, wipe the pan clean, and start over. Grind the salt and sesame seeds together, but you want to keep some texture to it, so don't grind so much that the seeds are completely powdered. This can be stored in an airtight container at room temperature for up to a year and offered as a table condiment.

5 To make the horseradish sour cream, simply place the kefir sour cream in a bowl and stir in the grated horseradish.

6 To serve, cut the baked sweet potatoes in half lengthwise. Scoop out about $1/3$ cup of flesh from each half into a medium bowl. Add the horseradish sour cream and a pinch of smoked paprika (if using). Mash until smooth, then season with salt and pepper. Spoon the mashed filling back into the sweet potato boats and top with a slice of avocado butter and a sprinkle of gomasio. Serve with the chili kale crisps on the side.

CHILI KALE CRISPS

When the dehydrator goes on to make kale chips, I make as much as I can—about four or five trays is as much as I can fit in at one time.

MAKES 1 X 1-QUART JAR OF CRISPS

$^1/_2$ cup cashews, soaked
I bunch of kale
$^1/_4$ cup olive oil
I tablespoon nutritional yeast
2 teaspoons raw apple cider vinegar or lemon juice
2 teaspoons onion powder
2 teaspoons smoked paprika
I teaspoon garlic powder
I teaspoon sea salt
$^1/_2$ teaspoon cayenne pepper

1 First soak the cashews in a bowl of water overnight. In the morning, drain and rinse the nuts.

2 Destem the kale and place it in a large bowl. Make a paste by blending the soaked cashews and all the other ingredients (except the kale) in a blender. Add this paste to the kale leaves and massage it into the leaves well by hand.

3 Arrange the kale on a dehydrator tray and dehydrate for 12 hours at 115°F. This can also be done in a fan-assisted oven at 175°F for four hours. Once they are crispy, you can store them in an airtight container for up to a month, if they last that long.

The Cultured Club burger

As a conscious consumer, blindly buying meat from a supermarket is part of a long story without a happy ending. In Ireland we are relatively lucky in that our landscape has fields with cows in them, so at least they are grass fed. If we pursue the story a little further, we can find farmers who are doing their best to deliver great meat, so if meat is your thing, seek out the story with a better beginning, middle, and end.

But the meat bit is an easy option. There are plenty of great vegetarian burgers that you can easily create at home, such as mushroom burgers, lentil burgers, eggplant burgers, and chickpea burgers. There is a balance to the flavor and the texture, so you don't feel shortchanged by something that resembles dry cardboard.

The first tip is that no matter what vegetables you're using, sauté them in a bit of oil or water first, until soft, then add them to the burger mix. Secondly, don't be shy with the spices—seasoning is a huge part of the flavor in a vegetarian burger.

As for the texture, liquid ingredients are added for moisture, but that doesn't mean they can't also add flavor. Soy sauce or tamari is a great choice, but think about adding some complex flavor with the vinegars you have created (see pages 318–325).

Leftover almond pulp from making almond milk can be used to make veggie burgers, as can vegetable pulp if juicing is your thing. Leftover rice, millet, buckwheat, or lentils can all find their way into a delicious blend too. If there are any mashed potatoes or sweet potatoes left over from dinner, use those up too!

It really can be this simple! Your efforts can even be frozen to use at a later date.

- **Build your base:** Try beets, carrots, lentils, chopped mushrooms, ground nuts, mashed potatoes, or roasted butternut squash.

- **Add a little flavor:** Spice blends, fresh herbs, tamari, miso, or nutritional yeast.

- **Stick it all together:** Flour, breadcrumbs, sticky grains, mashed sticky beans, tahini, nut butters, eggs, chia seeds, or flaxseeds. Sweeten with maple syrup if necessary.

- **To cook:** Crumb them up in a little polenta, milled nuts, or seeds, then bake or fry.

- **To serve:** You'll need some burger buns, crisp lettuce leaves, and sliced fresh vegetables. Top with caramelized onions (see page 232), some homemade carrot or cabbage slaw, spicy mustard, mayo, relish, guacamole, hummus, chutney, or any of the many dips on pages 111–128. Now go!

CHICKPEA BURGERS

Use whatever bread you like for these burgers: try flaxseed focaccia (page 157) or even grilled portobello mushroom "buns" or chargrilled eggplant slices—however you roll! **MAKES 2 BURGERS**

$1/2$ cup cooked or canned chickpeas, drained and rinsed

$1/2$ cup sautéed veggies (any veggies will do—see the note on page 238)

I egg, lightly beaten, or I tablespoon milled chia seeds soaked in 3 tablespoons filtered water

2 tablespoons chickpea flour

I tablespoon grated fresh ginger

$1/2$ tablespoon chopped fresh parsley

$1/4$ teaspoon ground cumin

$1/4$ teaspoon curry powder

Pinch of chili flakes

Sea salt and freshly ground black pepper

Coconut oil, for frying

TO SERVE:

Bread or burger buns

Lacto-fermented mayonnaise (page 115)

Baby salad leaves

1 Combine all the ingredients except the coconut oil in a food processor and pulse until blended but not completely pureed—you still want the burgers to have some texture.

2 Melt a little coconut oil in a pan set over a medium-high heat. Split the chickpea mixture in half and form into two round burgers. Cook for three to five minutes, until golden, then carefully turn over and cook on the other side for a few more minutes, until golden.

3 Toast your bread and slather with mayonnaise. Pile on some salad leaves and top with a chickpea burger.

BEAN PASTE

I generally start with great intentions for bean dishes and then find I have soaked and prepared way too much. This is a great way to make use of leftover beans, with the extra bonus of making them even more nutritious. Quesadillas, here we come! You can pull out the tomato salsa on page 82. I've had the best results with black beans, red kidney beans, and pinto beans.

MAKES 1 X 1-PINT JAR

I cup cooked or canned beans of your choice (see the note above)
....
I red onion, roughly chopped
....
3 to 6 garlic cloves (preferably fermented—see page 68), peeled
....
4 tablespoons whey, brine, or sauerkraut juice
....
I tablespoon sea salt

1 If you're cooking your beans from scratch over the convenience of buying canned, you will need to start with $1/2$ cup of dried beans and soak them first overnight. Most varieties should be soaked for eight hours before cooking, so cover them with plenty of water, making sure they are covered by at least 2 inches of water.

2 Once soaked, drain the beans and place in a large saucepan with sufficient fresh water for them to have room to move about. Cook them on a gentle simmer for about 30 minutes, until they are creamy in the center but not split or burst.

3 Allow them to cool in the cooking water, as straining them will cause the skins to shrivel. You can store the beans in the fridge in their cooking liquid for up to one week.

4 To make the paste, put the onion and garlic in a food processor or blender and give it a whirl until well chopped. If you have fermented garlic cloves, using them will add extra probiotics to the party. Add the cooked beans, whey, and salt and blend until smooth.

5 Place in a clean wide-mouthed pint jar, making sure you leave 1 inch of headspace at the top of the jar. Cover tightly and leave at room temperature for about three days before transferring to the fridge, where this will keep for two months.

MASALA QUINOA CROQUETTES WITH INDIAN CAULIFLOWER AND MANGO CHUTNEY

With Indian spices and your fine collection of fermented Indian accompaniments, you might want to make more than eight of these—just saying! They are flavorful on the palate, a perfect snack, starter, or addition to a main meal. Anything that offers an interesting texture variation is always a good thing. **MAKES 8 CROQUETTES**

I sweet potato

$1/3$ cup quinoa

I egg, lightly beaten, or I tablespoon milled flaxseeds soaked in 2 tablespons filtered water

I small onion, finely diced

I garlic clove, finely chopped

2-inch piece of fresh ginger, peeled and finely chopped

A few sprigs of fresh cilantro, finely chopped

$1/2$ teaspoon garam masala

$1/2$ teaspoon curry powder

$1/2$ teaspoon sea salt

$1/4$ teaspoon mustard seeds

$1/8$ teaspoon cayenne pepper

Melted coconut oil, for brushing the croquettes

TO SERVE:

Lime pickle (page 98)

Indian-spiced lacto-fermented cauliflower (page 72)

Mango chutney (page 107)

1 Preheat the oven to 390°F. Line a large baking tray with parchment paper.

2 This is the lazy way to cook a sweet potato—just prick it with a fork three or four times and place it directly on the oven rack. Place a sheet of foil over the bottom of the oven to catch any syrup from the sweet potato that might drip out as it cooks. Bake for 45 minutes or up to an hour if it's large, until cooked through and tender. When it's done, turn off the oven but let it sit in the warm oven for at least 30 minutes. I tend to make good use of the cooking time and make extra, as these can be stored by removing the skin and popping them into a sealed container in the fridge for up to three days. For example, you could make a few extra for the sweet potato boats on page 235.

3 Meanwhile, cook the quinoa. (I always like to make a little extra quinoa, as it keeps for a few days in the fridge and can be easily whipped up into a nutritious meal, such as the Thai bowl on page 251.) To make the perfect quinoa, first you will need to rinse it to get rid of its bitter protective coating. Place the quinoa in a fine-mesh sieve and run it under cold water for a few seconds. Place the rinsed quinoa in a saucepan and cover with twice the amount of liquid. Bring this to a boil, then reduce the heat and simmer for 15 minutes, until all the liquid has been absorbed. Use a fork to fluff it up and separate the grains.

4 Cut the sweet potato in half lengthwise and scoop the flesh out into a large bowl. Mash well, then add the cooked quinoa and all the remaining ingredients except the oil and mix until well combined. Form the mixture into eight croquettes and place on the lined baking tray. Brush the top of the croquettes with a little melted coconut oil.

5 Bake for 15 minutes, then remove from the oven, turn the croquettes over, and brush the other side with coconut oil. Bake for another 15 minutes, until golden brown. Serve with lime pickle, Indian-spiced lacto-fermented cauliflower, and mango chutney.

VIETNAMESE PANCAKES WITH KIMCHI

Never mind the flavor—when you see how vibrantly yellow these pancakes are, you will feel the benefits with every mouthful. Plus it's another great excuse to eat kimchi. **MAKES 4 PANCAKES**

1¼ cup rice flour

1 small egg, lightly beaten

1 teaspoon ground turmeric

½ teaspoon sea salt

1¾ cups (1 x 13.5-ounce can) coconut milk

1 tablespoon coconut oil, for cooking

½ pound kimchi

¼ pound mung bean sprouts

¼ cup mixed black and white sesame seeds

½ bunch of fresh cilantro, chopped

½ bunch of fresh mint, chopped

Handful of fresh Thai basil, chopped

Sesame oil, for drizzling

Pinch of black pepper

1 First make the batter. Put the rice flour, egg, turmeric, and salt in a bowl. Slowly pour in the coconut milk, whisking to avoid lumps. You're after a thin crêpe batter, so add more coconut milk (or water) if necessary. Set aside to rest.

2 Melt the coconut oil in a large non-stick frying pan over a medium heat. Pour in a quarter of the batter and swirl it around to coat the pan. The edges can be thinner than the center, which means they'll be crispy. Once the underside is golden brown, flip the pancake over and cook the other side. Remove and keep warm while you make the remaining pancakes.

3 To serve, place a warm pancake on a serving dish and pile the kimchi, bean sprouts, sesame seeds, and herbs on top. Drizzle with sesame oil, season with a pinch of freshly ground black pepper and serve.

TAMAGOYAKI (JAPANESE EGG ROLL) WITH DAIKON RADISH KIMCHI

This omelet is so full of flavor that you will find it hard to go back to regular omelets as you once knew them. **SERVES 2**

3 large eggs

3 tablespoons dashi (page 180)

1 teaspoon raw cane sugar

1 teaspoon tamari

1 teaspoon mirin

2 pinches of sea salt

2 tablespoons melted coconut oil

1¹/₂ sheets of nori (optional)

Daikon radish kimchi (page 45), to serve

1 Crack the eggs into a bowl and gently whisk.

2 Combine the dashi, sugar, tamari, mirin and salt in a separate bowl and mix well. Pour the seasonings mixture into the eggs and whisk gently.

3 Heat a pan over a medium heat. Dip a folded piece of paper towel in the oil and wipe the pan with the oiled paper towel—this is the key to evenly distribute the oil. When the pan is hot, pour a thin layer of the egg mixture in the pan, tilting to cover the bottom of the pan. You should hear it sizzle.

4 After the bottom of the egg has set but the top is still soft, start rolling the omelet into a log shape. If you like, you can put half a sheet of nori on top of the omelet before you roll it up.

5 Move the rolled omelet to the side of the pan to keep it warm. Apply a little more oil to the pan with the paper towel, including under the omelet. Pour another thin layer of the egg mixture into the pan, covering the bottom of the pan again but this time making sure to lift up the omelet to spread the mixture underneath. When the new layer of egg has set and is still soft on top, start rolling it up again, just as you did before. Add another sheet of nori, if using, before rolling up the omelet.

6 Repeat these steps until you have used up all your egg mixture. If you want to achieve egg roll perfection, transfer the hot egg roll onto a sushi mat and shape while it's still hot.

7 To serve, cut the egg roll into slices $1/2$-inch thick. Keep it simple and serve with some daikon radish kimchi.

MOROCCAN TAGINE WITH PRESERVED LEMONS

You can use almost any kind of vegetables in this stew. It's perfect for emptying the fridge. **SERVES 4**

3 tablespoons olive oil

I large onion, roughly chopped

3 garlic cloves, finely chopped

I-inch piece of fresh ginger, peeled and finely chopped, or I teaspoon ground ginger

I to 2 tablespoons ground cinnamon

I teaspoon ground cumin

Pinch of sea salt

³/₄ cup canned chopped tomatoes

¹/₂ cup harissa

Zest and juice of I lemon

Handful of fresh cilantro, chopped

3 carrots, cut into bite-sized chunks

I sweet potato, peeled and cut into bite-sized chunks

¹/₂ small pumpkin or butternut squash, peeled and cut into bite-sized chunks

I zucchini, cut into bite-sized chunks

Handful of dried apricots, chopped (optional)

¹/₂ cup cooked or canned chickpeas, drained and rinsed

I cup quinoa

TO SERVE:

Preserved lemons (page 97), chopped

Chopped roasted almonds

Chopped fresh cilantro

Chopped fresh mint

Moroccan carrots (page 59)

Moroccan kraut (page 38)

1 Heat the olive oil in a large saucepan over a medium heat. Add the onion and sauté for a few minutes, until it softens. Add the garlic, ginger, spices, and a pinch of salt and stir around for a minute before adding the tomatoes, harissa, lemon juice, and fresh cilantro. Bring to a boil, then lower the heat.

2 Add the carrots, sweet potato, pumpkin, zucchini, and apricots (if using). Stir around, making sure all the vegetables are somewhat covered in tomato sauce. Put the lid on and simmer for about an hour, stirring carefully once or twice. When the vegetables are tender, add the cooked chickpeas and let everything simmer for five minutes.

3 Meanwhile, cook the quinoa. (I always like to make a little extra quinoa, as it keeps for a few days in the fridge and can be easily whipped up into a nutritious meal, such as the Thai bowl on page 251.) To make the perfect quinoa, first you will need to rinse it to get rid of its bitter protective coating. Place the quinoa in a fine-mesh sieve and run it under cold water for a few seconds. Place the rinsed quinoa in a saucepan and cover with twice the amount of liquid. Bring this to a boil, then reduce the heat and simmer for 15 minutes, until all the liquid has been absorbed. Use a fork to fluff it up and separate the grains.

4 Serve the tagine with the cooked quinoa and top with a squeeze of lemon juice, a pinch of lemon zest, chopped preserved lemons, chopped roasted almonds, fresh cilantro, and fresh mint. Add a generous topping of Moroccan carrots and Moroccan kraut for some extra zing.

THAI BOWL WITH A QUICK THAI NUT SAUCE

Leftover quinoa gets a sudden transformation in this quick dish. The nutty flavor of the quinoa is enhanced by the creamy nut sauce. **SERVES 2**

I cup quinoa

Juice of I lemon

I red pepper, finely chopped

1/2 bunch of spring onions, finely chopped

I cup krishna kraut (page 39)

1/2 cup activated or toasted cashews, chopped

1/2 bunch of fresh cilantro, finely chopped

FOR THE THAI NUT SAUCE:

1/2 cup coconut milk

1/4 cup creamy almond butter

3 garlic cloves, minced

3 tablespoons filtered water

3 tablespoons lime-flavored water kefir (page 280) or 1/4 preserved lime

3 tablespoons tamari or coconut aminos

I tablespoon finely chopped fresh ginger

I tablespoon fish sauce (optional)

I teaspoon Tabasco sauce

1 To make the perfect quinoa, first you will need to rinse it to get rid of its bitter protective coating. Place the quinoa in a fine-mesh sieve and run it under cold water for a few seconds. Place the rinsed quinoa in a saucepan and cover with twice the amount of liquid. Bring this to a boil, then reduce the heat and simmer for 15 minutes, until all the liquid has been absorbed. Use a fork to fluff it up and separate the grains, then mix in the lemon juice.

2 Meanwhile, to make the nut sauce, place all the ingredients in a blender or food processor and blend until creamy.

3 Assemble all the prepared ingredients in wide bowls, starting with the quinoa, then top with red pepper, spring onions, and sauerkraut. Drizzle the nut sauce generously over the Thai bowl, sprinkle with the cashews and cilantro, and serve.

HOMEMADE TEMPEH

When your kitchen has found its rhythm and you're ready to transition from easy lacto-ferments to using starters you can't pronounce, give this a try. Once you have mastered this method you can try other combinations using a variety of beans, such as pinto beans, black beans, or chickpeas, and various cooked grains, such as quinoa, millet, and rice. **SERVES 4**

5^1/$_2$ cups dry soybeans

4 tablespoons rice vinegar

2 teaspoons tempeh starter (available online or at your local health food store)

1 First boil the soybeans for about an hour, until soft, then drain and rinse the cooked beans. Place them in a food processor fitted with the slicing blade and pulse to remove the outer skin and split the beans.

2 Pop the beans in a bowl with water to enable you to easily remove the hulls from the beans. Once separated, drain and pat the beans dry with a clean tea towel to remove any excess water.

3 Pierce two ziplock bags all over with a sewing needle to create tiny holes spaced about ^{1}/$_2$-inch apart.

4 Put the beans back into the mixing bowl. Add the vinegar and starter and mix thoroughly, then divide the mixture between the ziplock bags, making sure they are only half full and the tempeh is no more than 1-inch thick. Place the bags on a towel and lay the bags out flat, then put them in your dehydrator set at 85–90°F. It's vital to maintain a consistent temperature throughout the cooking process.

5 After 15 to 16 hours, there will be condensation on the bags and the bags will also begin generating their own heat. At 21 to 22 hours, you will begin to see the white mycelium. At 24 to 26 hours, these will have turned gray—congratulations! Your tempeh is done and ready to eat.

6 You can either eat the tempeh fresh, refrigerate it for up to five days, or freeze it for up to a year.

MARINATED TEMPEH WITH CARROT AND ZUCCHINI NOODLES

If you have made your own tempeh, well done! There is no comparison in taste and self-satisfaction. I do resort to shop-bought sometimes, though, but this delicious marinade forgives all. **SERVES 2**

2 zucchinis

2 carrots

1 x ¹/₂-pound block of plain tempeh (page 252 or shop-bought)

4 cups filtered water

¹/₂ cup tamari or liquid aminos

3 tablespoons coconut oil

2 garlic cloves, minced

4 tablespoons unpasteurized brown rice miso or chickpea miso

2 tablespoons minced fresh ginger

2 tablespoons pure maple syrup

Black and white sesame seeds, to garnish

FOR THE CARROT AND GINGER DRESSING:

¹/₂ pound carrots, peeled and chopped into chunks

¹/₄ small red onion, quartered

1 garlic clove, crushed (optional)

¹/₂ cup neutral oil like mild olive oil or grapeseed oil

¹/₄ cup kombucha vinegar (page 318)

2 tablespoons tamari or liquid aminos

2 tablespoons fermented ginger (page 63)

1 tablespoon toasted sesame oil

Sea salt and freshly ground black pepper

1 Prepare your zucchinis and carrots in a spiralizer to create noodles. You can also use a standard vegetable peeler to create ribbons if a spiralizer isn't one of your kitchen gadgets. Place in a bowl and set aside.

2 To make the dressing, place all the ingredients together in a blender and whiz until smooth, then pour it over the noodles, coating them evenly. Set aside.

3 Put the whole block of tempeh in a large saucepan with the water and six tablespoons of the tamari. Bring to a boil, then reduce the heat to medium and cook for 15 minutes. Transfer the tempeh to a plate and let it cool for ten minutes. (Reserve the cooking liquid for another use, such as a noodle soup base or to cook rice with.) Once cooled, cut it into bite-sized cubes.

4 Melt the coconut oil in a large frying pan over a medium heat. Once the oil shimmers, add the tempeh and cook, stirring frequently, until it's golden brown on all sides.

5 Meanwhile, whisk together the remaining two tablespoons of tamari with the minced garlic, miso, ginger, and maple syrup in a small bowl. Add to the browned tempeh in the frying pan, stirring to blend and coat.

6 To serve, place a nest of noodles in a bowl. Top with a serving of tempeh and garnish with black and white sesame seeds.

FERMENTED TEFF FLATBREAD (INJERA)

Traditionally these are served with a lentil stew or dal. I've given you two options on pages 257–259, so if you make a double batch of the batter, that can be two midweek dinners done. **MAKES 4 PANCAKES**

1³/₄ cups teff flour
....
I cup filtered water
....
¹/₄ teaspoon sea salt, or more to taste
....
¹/₂ teaspoon baking powder
....
Coconut oil

1 Place the teff flour in a large glass bowl, add the water, and stir well. Cover with a clean tea towel and place on the counter for 24 hours. Do not agitate or stir during this time.

2 After 24 hours, you'll see that your batter is alive and bubbling due to the fermentation. Stir in the salt, followed by the baking powder. Your batter will deflate when you stir it.

3 Put a little coconut oil on a cloth or a piece of paper towel and lightly coat a frying pan with the oil. Set the pan over a medium heat, then pour enough batter into the pan to thinly cover the entire surface, which should be roughly a quarter of the batter. Cover with a lid—this is important because you want to keep a lot of moisture in the pan. Cook for five to seven minutes. You'll see bubbles on the top, like pancakes, and the batter will have started to dry out. When the top is dry and the edges begin to curl, use a spatula to remove the injera from the pan—you don't need to flip it over. Repeat until you have used up all the batter, wiping the pan with the oiled paper towel between each pancake. Serve with one of the options on pages 257–259.

LEMON DAL WITH INJERA AND COCONUT CHUTNEY

I love my slow cooker. After a year of living without a stovetop I became well versed in the skill of soaking my grains and pulses the night before and then throwing everything into the slow cooker in the morning and switching it on to a low heat. You can take this route if you have a slow cooker or you can go about it the long way outlined below. **SERVES 4**

2 cups red or green lentils

6 garlic cloves

I tablespoon grated fresh ginger

I tablespoon chili powder

I¹/₂ teaspoons ground turmeric

¹/₃ cup lemon juice

Sea salt

¹/₂ cup ghee or coconut oil

6 dried chilies or I teaspoon chili flakes

I tablespoon cumin seeds

Chopped fresh cilantro, to garnish

Injera (page 256), to serve

Coconut chutney (page 107), to serve

1 Soak the lentils in filtered water for about eight hours or overnight.

2 Drain the lentils and place in a medium saucepan with 4 cups of fresh filtered water. Add two cloves of minced garlic along with the ginger, chili powder, and turmeric. Bring to a boil, then reduce the heat and let it simmer for 25 to 30 minutes, until the lentils are soft. Add the lemon juice and salt to taste.

3 Meanwhile, melt the ghee in a pan on a high heat. Add the remaining garlic cloves along with the dried chilies and cumin seeds. Cook for about five minutes, until the garlic is beginning to blister. Remove from the heat and allow to cool just a little, then pour the flavored oil over the lentils.

4 Spoon the lemon dal into warmed bowls and garnish with chopped fresh cilantro. Serve with the injera on the side and some coconut chutney.

SPICY ETHIOPIAN LENTILS WITH INJERA

I am becoming more and more convinced that flatbreads are the perfect eating utensil, and this traditional spicy stew will give you the opportunity to practice. The berbere spice blend is at the heart of the dish, with instant fragrant and spicy appeal. **SERVES 4**

2 cups red lentils

4 tablespoons coconut oil

I red onion, diced

4 garlic cloves, minced

3 tablespoons paprika

2 teaspoons chili powder

2 teaspoons ground cumin

I teaspoon ground coriander

I teaspoon ground cardamom

I teaspoon fenugreek seeds, crushed

I teaspoon ground ginger

I teaspoon ground turmeric

I teaspoon fine sea salt

I teaspoon freshly ground black pepper

$1/2$ teaspoon ground cinnamon

$1/2$ teaspoon allspice

$1/4$ teaspoon ground cloves

$1/2$ lime, juiced

TO SERVE:

Chopped fresh cilantro

Sweet and spicy onion relish (page 7I)

Injera (page 256)

1 Bring a pot of water to a boil. Add the lentils, reduce the heat to a simmer, and cook for about ten minutes. Red lentils cook considerably faster than any other lentil. Once cooked, drain and set aside.

2 Melt the coconut oil in a large pan set over a medium heat. Add the onion and sauté for about five minutes, then add the garlic and cook for another two minutes. Add all the spices to form a heady paste. This spice blend is called berbere, a cornerstone of Ethiopian cooking.

3 Mix the cooked, drained lentils into the onion and spice paste together with 2 cups filtered water. Bring to a gentle simmer and cook until the water has been absorbed and the dish has a stew-like consistency. Finish with the lime juice.

4 Garnish with chopped fresh cilantro and serve with sweet and spicy onion relish, mopping up every morsel with the injera flatbread.

FALAFEL WITH HUMMUS AND BABA GHANOUSH

I cannot resist the satisfaction of falafel. While it's nearly perfect for my taste buds, I still need the tang to ensure that my food is "alive" and abundant in raw living goodness. **SERVES 4 TO 6**

³/₄ cup walnuts or pecans

2 cups cooked or canned chickpeas, rinsed, drained, and patted dry

I garlic clove, minced

2 tablespoons fresh parsley, chopped

2 tablespoons fresh mint leaves, chopped

2 tablespoons fresh cilantro, chopped

3 tablespoons lemon juice

3 tablespoons tahini

2 tablespoons olive oil

2 tablespoons coconut sugar

I tablespoon ground flaxseed

I¹/₂ teaspoons sea salt

¹/₄ teaspoon chili flakes

2 cardamom pods, crushed and green shells discarded (optional)

¹/₂ tablespoon cumin seeds

¹/₂ teaspoon mustard seeds

3 tablespoons sesame seeds, for coating

3 tablespoons hemp seeds or 6 tablespoons polenta, for coating

TO SERVE:

Pink pickled turnips (page 60)

Thinly sliced fresh radishes

Cucumber slices or ribbons

Greek yogurt

Lime juice

Lemony hummus (page I20)

Fermented baba ghanoush (page 85)

1 Preheat the oven to 375°F. Line two baking trays with parchment paper.

2 Place the nuts in a food processor and grind into a coarse meal. Add the chickpeas, garlic, fresh herbs, lemon juice, tahini, olive oil, sugar, ground flaxseed, salt, and chili flakes.

3 Grind the cardamom, cumin, and mustard seeds in a mortar and pestle or spice grinder, then add them to the food processor. Process everything until well combined, scraping down the sides of the food processor if needed. Take care not to puree the mixture—it should remain somewhat chunky.

4 Place the sesame seeds and hemp seeds or polenta in separate bowls or plates. Form the falafel into balls, rolling each ball in the seed or polenta coating, then place on the lined trays.

5 Bake in the oven for 15 minutes, turning the falafel every five minutes to achieve an even color.

6 Serve the falafel with the pickled turnips, fresh radishes, and cucumbers. Mix together some Greek yogurt and a little freshly squeezed lime juice and serve on the side along with separate small bowls of hummus and baba ghanoush.

DESSERTS

DESSERT IS REALLY where my quest for healthy food began in earnest. Many years back, I needed to upskill and learn how to make sweet treats that didn't seem to be loaded with sugar, refined flours, sprinkles, syrups, frostings, and all manner of things I would never consider eating, let alone feed my children. Family life was going to need it.

Raw food desserts became my kitchen hobby and the many options passed with approval. It was a tough call, though, as the children needed convincing—they cannot be duped, especially when it comes to sugar. (Thank you, Mother Nature, for water kefir to mop up the sugar indulgences.)

I think it's probably fair to say that you might need some convincing too. I'm guessing you haven't really considered fermented food for dessert before now, and to be honest, it was a slow progression for me too. But seeing as many desserts rely on milk, yogurts, or cream, making them as a "cultured" version was a natural step. The tart tang of a cultured ingredient can be balanced out with something sweet—sometimes all it takes is a little vanilla.

While I do still enjoy a sweet treat, I rarely have them and they're not something I crave. I have about three favorite desserts, so this is only a short selection of recipes, mostly dedicated to my children, who always give me more than honest feedback. My desire for sweets has diminished radically and my palate is highly sensitive to them now. If you taste my kombucha, you'll see what I mean! What often seems overly sweet and "not quite there yet" to me is a glass full of vinegar to most.

But these desserts are a win-win: you get your sweet treat and your bacterial ecosystem also gets a dose of good bacteria to crowd out the sugar-loving kind. As the beneficial bacteria begin to dominate, sugar cravings will dissipate.

FUDGE ICE POPS ESPECIALLY FOR THE KIDDIES

Bananas make a great base for ice cream and their natural sweetness can carry many flavors. To freeze bananas for ice cream, peel and chop them before placing them in a container or ziplock bag in the freezer. Combining some tart kefir in the mix is a great way to sneak some probiotics into kids' tummies.

MAKES 4 TO 6 POPS

2 bananas, peeled, chopped, and frozen

1 to 1¼ cups coconut milk kefir (page 144)

1 cup water kefir (page 280), sweet kombucha (page 302), or jun (page 312)

2 tablespoons cacao powder

¼ teaspoon vanilla extract

Pinch of sea salt

1 to 2 tablespoons coconut oil, melted

Place all the ingredients except for the coconut oil into a blender. Puree until smooth, then slowly drizzle in the coconut oil until blended. Pour the mixture into popsicle molds and freeze until firm.

BANANA ICE CREAM WITH SALTED CARAMEL SAUCE

I have always been drawn to sweet potatoes, knowing they hold more potential than their savory appearance would lead us to believe. However, I'd never gotten around to making an actual dessert from them until I stumbled across a recipe for a caramel sauce made from sweet potato. Credit for the original recipe goes to Brad Leone of Bon Appétit *magazine, but put the word "salted" in front of a caramel sauce and I cannot resist! Enter the fermented sweet potato salted caramel sauce.* **MAKES ABOUT ¼ CUP OF SAUCE**

3¹/₃ pounds sweet potatoes, peeled and cut into quarters
....
I cup filtered water
....
4 bananas, peeled, chopped, and frozen

1 Preheat the oven to 390°F.

2 Place the chopped potatoes and ¹/₂ cup of the water in a 9-by-13-inch baking dish. Cover with tin foil and bake for one hour. Remove the foil and bake for 15 minutes more, uncovered. Remove the dish from the oven and add the remaining ¹/₂ cup of water to loosen up any bits stuck to the baking dish.

3 Place all the solids and liquids into a strainer lined with cheesecloth. Let this drain into a saucepan and cool for 30 minutes. Once it's cool enough to handle, squeeze as much liquid from the potatoes in the cheesecloth as possible. You should end up with about 1²/₃ cups of liquid. (Use the sweet potato solids remaining in the cloth by adding it to a hummus or mixing it with some harissa for an interesting dip.)

4 Bring the sweet potato liquid to a boil in a saucepan, then reduce the heat to a steady simmer. Allow the liquid to reduce for 15 to 20 minutes, until it starts to thicken and form a caramel. Stir often in the final minutes to avoiding burning. Pour into a jar and store in the refrigerator for up to two weeks.

5 To make the ice cream, place the frozen bananas in a food processor fitted with the S-blade or a Vitamix blender and begin to process. You may need to pulse it a few times to get it going, but once the bananas are broken down they will begin to turn smooth and creamy. Process until there are no lumps. Once you're there, scoop into bowls and serve with the caramel sauce drizzled over.

VANILLA KEFIR ICE CREAM

I thought it was worth investing in a cheap-ish ice cream maker for the sake of getting it right for my two ice cream-loving children. But what if you don't have an ice cream maker? It can still be done. Like everything worthwhile, it just takes a little bit longer. **MAKES 1 QUART**

2 eggs

¹/₂ cup raw honey

2 cups milk kefir (page 134), yogurt, or buttermilk

I cup cultured cream (page 142)

2 teaspoons vanilla extract

1 Beat the eggs together well, then beat in the honey. Blend in the kefir, cultured cream, and vanilla. Taste the mix, keeping in mind that the finished ice cream will be slightly less sweet than the kefir mixture before it's frozen, and add more sweetener if necessary. Transfer to an ice cream maker and freeze according to the manufacturer's instructions. (For me, that means adding the mixture to the pre-frozen bowl of the machine while it's running and letting it churn for 20 to 25 minutes.)

2 If you don't have an ice cream maker, pour the ice cream mixture into a plastic bowl and put it in the freezer for about two hours, until frozen. Remove from the freezer and allow to soften slightly, then break it up and put it in your blender. Blend until creamy, but not too long or it will melt. You just want to break up the ice crystals that are beginning to form. Place it back in the freezer for another two hours to firm up again, then blend again. The ice cream should be thick. Return it to the freezer one last time to firm up, then enjoy.

3 Alternatively, if you don't have a blender either, you can check the ice cream every 45 minutes, and as it starts to freeze near the edges, remove it from the freezer and stir vigorously to break up those ice crystals. You are the churn that is otherwise part of an ice cream machine! Return it to the freezer and continue to check it every 30 minutes (you might need to set an alarm for this step to help you remember), stirring vigorously every time it's starting to freeze. Repeat this step every 30 minutes about three more times. You'll deserve your ice cream by then!

MINT CHOCOLATE ICE CREAM

As kefir is perfect for flavoring at the secondary fermentation stage, you can really play around with the flavor potential—such as mint, my kids' favorite! **MAKES 1 QUART**

3²/₃ cups full-fat coconut milk kefir (page 144)

¹/₂ cup raw honey, plus more if necessary

2 teaspoons organic peppermint extract

I teaspoon organic vanilla extract (optional)

3 ounces dark chocolate, shaved

1 In a medium-sized bowl, whisk together the coconut milk, honey, and the peppermint and vanilla extracts. Add the dark chocolate shavings and mix through. Freeze in an ice cream maker according to the manufacturer's instructions.

2 If you don't have an ice cream maker, pour the mixture into a plastic bowl and put it in the freezer just until frozen. Remove from the freezer and allow to soften slightly, then break it up and put it in your blender. Blend until creamy, but not too long or it will melt.

VEGAN COCONUT LIME ICE CREAM

Anything with lime works for me. Make it ice-cold and you have a perfect treat for a hot day. Adding avocados to this ice cream nearly makes it too healthy to even it call ice cream. **MAKES 1 QUART**

2 avocados, halved, stoned, and flesh scooped out

I cup coconut milk kefir (page 144)

I cup maple syrup

¹/₂ cup freshly squeezed lime juice (about 5 limes)

¹/₄ cup coconut water

I tablespoon lime zest

1 Place all the ingredients in a blender or food processor and blend until smooth, scraping down the sides of the bowl a couple times for a really smooth texture. Pour into an ice cream maker and freeze according to the manufacturer's instructions. Serve immediately or freeze for a firmer texture.

2 If you don't have an ice cream maker, pour the mixture into a plastic bowl and put it in the freezer just until frozen. Remove from the freezer and allow to soften slightly, then break it up and put it in your blender. Blend until creamy, but not too long or it will melt.

CULTURED APPLE AND GOJI BERRY COMPOTE WITH TOASTED BUCKWHEAT AND COCONUT YOGURT

Provided you have all these wonderful jars of cultured goodness on hand, this is the quickest, tastiest dessert to assemble. I would even say it could pass as a breakfast too, it's that good. **SERVES 4 TO 6**

5 medium organic apples, unpeeled, cored, and halved

2 oranges, peeled

3 tablespoons coconut sugar

2 teaspoons ground cinnamon

1 teaspoon grated fresh ginger

^{1}/$_2$ teaspoon unrefined sea salt

1 cup filtered water

4 tablespoons whey or kombucha vinegar (page 318)

^{1}/$_2$ cup goji berries

Coconut yogurt, to serve

Toasted buckwheat groats (kasha) or buckwheat crispies (page 174), to serve

1 Pop two apple halves in a high-speed blender along with the peeled oranges, coconut sugar, cinnamon, ginger, salt, and water and blend for about one minute, until smooth. Transfer to a large bowl and stir in the whey or kombucha vinegar.

2 Chop the remaining apples and add to the bowl along with the goji berries.

3 Spoon the apple and goji berry compote into a clean 1-quart jar and mash down so that the apples release their juices and are completely covered with the liquid. Leave at least 1 inch of headspace at the top of the jar to allow the compote to expand, then cover with a lid.

4 Ferment the compote at room temperature for two days, then store in the refrigerator for up to two weeks. Fermented fruits don't keep for long and this will start to turn quite alcoholic after two weeks.

5 To serve, spoon the compote into small serving bowls. Top with a generous dollop of coconut yogurt and sprinkle with some toasted buckwheat groats or buckwheat crispies.

THE CULTURED CLUB'S CHOCOLATE CELEBRATION CAKE

My first real epiphany in the dessert realm was making raw cakes. It was a natural step that I should make them even more digestible by using fermented nuts in the filling, making the cakes lighter and even easier to digest. The Cultured Club's chocolate celebration cake has been known to take on many forms and flavors. **SERVES 8**

FOR THE CRUST:

1¹/₈ cups whole raw almonds

¹/₄ cup cacao powder or unsweetened cocoa powder

¹/₂ cup dates, pitted and chopped, plus more as needed

FOR THE FILLING:

1 pound fermented cashew nut cheese (see the recipe on page 151, but use cashews instead of macadamias and omit the nutritional yeast)

¹/₂ cup coconut sugar or xylitol, or ¹/₃ cup maple syrup

¹/₃ cup cacao powder or unsweetened cocoa powder

1 cup freshly squeezed orange juice

1 cup melted coconut oil

1 teaspoon finely grated orange zest

¹/₄ teaspoon orange extract

Pinch of sea salt

1 To make the crust, process the almonds to a powder in the food processor. Add the cacao powder and blend again. (You can add in a few other superfoods now, such as maca, camu camu, and some cacao nibs, but this is optional.) Add the dates gradually and process until the mixture starts to come together as a sticky dough. You might need a few more dates to help it bind together.

2 Line an 8-inch springform cake pan with plastic wrap and press the dough evenly into the bottom of the tin. Place it in the freezer to harden while you make your filling.

3 Put all the filling ingredients into a high-speed blender and blend until ultra-smooth. Grab your base from the freezer and pour the filling into the pan, spreading it evenly over the base. Put in the freezer for one hour to set—if you can wait that long. Any leftovers (what leftovers?) will keep in the freezer for a month.

GRAIN-FREE KEFIR BROWNIES

There have been many best-ever brownie recipes since their invention well over 100 years ago, but this is another contender. With their fine profile of ingredients, what could go wrong? **MAKES 16 BROWNIES**

1¼ cups coconut flour

½ cup raw cacao powder

4 eggs, beaten

2 cups milk kefir (page 134)

1 tablespoon vanilla extract

1 teaspoon coconut sugar

1 teaspoon baking soda

¼ teaspoon sea salt

1 pound dark chocolate (at least 70 percent cocoa solids), broken into chunks

1 Preheat the oven to 350°F.

2 In a large bowl, combine all the ingredients except the chocolate chunks and mix well, then add the chocolate chunks and mix again. Line an 8-inch square brownie pan with parchment paper and add the batter into the lined pan, smoothing it out level with the back of the spatula.

3 Bake for 30 to 40 minutes or until the top is cracked and the sides are slightly firm yet a little soft in the middle of the pan. Remove from the oven and cool completely in the tray before cutting into squares.

COCONUT FLOUR CRÊPES

I love making homemade mayonnaise, but how I hate having all those egg whites to use up! I'm not tempted by meringues, nor do I like egg white omelets. In fact, every suggestion for using up egg whites was downright wrong for me until I discovered that you could pair them with coconut flour and sweeten them up. Bingo! **MAKES 4 TO 5 CRÊPES**

$^3/_4$ cup egg whites (approx. 6 large eggs)

2 tablespoons coconut flour

$^1/_2$ teaspoon arrowroot powder

$^1/_2$ teaspoon raw honey, maple syrup, or coconut sugar

Pinch of ground cinnamon

Coconut oil, for cooking

FOR THE TOPPING:

Coconut yogurt

Warmed berries

Toasted chopped almonds

Cacao nibs

Raw honey

Fresh mint

Coconut sugar

1 Blend together all the batter ingredients except the coconut oil in a blender. Set aside for 15 minutes.

2 Heat a frying pan over a medium heat. Once hot, melt $^1/_4$ teaspoon of coconut oil in the pan. Pour $^1/_4$ cup of batter into the pan, then reduce the heat and cook for two to three minutes, until the sides start to lift up. Flip over and cook for 20 to 30 seconds more, then transfer to a plate and keep warm. Continue until all the batter is used up, adding more coconut oil if the pan dries out.

3 To serve, spread the crêpes with coconut yogurt and top with warm berries, almonds, cacao nibs, and a drizzle of honey to serve. Garnish with fresh mint and sprinkle with coconut sugar.

FRUIT ROLL-UPS

You'll make these for your children with the best of intentions, but then end up eating them all yourself before your kids even get near them! They may seem like a lot of effort, but they are also a lot of fun and a joint kitchen project for many hands. **MAKES 2 TO 3 SHEETS OF FRUIT LEATHER**

$^3/_4$ cup fresh or frozen raspberries

2 cups coconut milk kefir (page 144)

1 to 2 tablespoons raw honey

1 teaspoon vanilla extract

1 Put all the ingredients in a blender or food processor and blend until smooth. Cover two or three dehydrator trays with Teflex sheets, then spread the mixture thinly over the lined trays. Dehydrate at 110°F for six to eight hours.

2 When dried, cut into strips and store in an airtight container for up to one month in the cupboard or up to a year in the freezer.

FERMENTED BEVERAGES

THE FAMILIAR FERMENTED beverages of beer, cider, and wine were my only understanding of fermentation until the wonderful world of fermentation for health presented itself to me. Oddly, I was never really interested in brewing my own alcohol, probably because I really understood how lethally alcoholic it can get after years of sip-testing my father's mead. It's easier than you think to brew something that would leave you catatonic!

There is a whole world of fermented drinks that are non-alcoholic. But I lie a little—although the process of fermentation in this case favors the production of lactic acid bacteria, there is a tiny amount of alcohol produced, but never any more than 0.5 percent. If it were more, don't you think we'd all know about kefirs and kombuchas on a par with beer and wine?

When brewing fermented drinks, the same rules apply to handling the grains and equipment as to any other ferment. Make sure all surfaces, bottles, and utensils are clean. It's sufficient to wash equipment with boiling water, and see page 24 for tips on how to sterilize your jars.

When bottling these drinks after the initial fermentation, make sure you choose sturdy, heavy-bottomed bottles. There have been instances of "bottle bombs" exploding, sending glass shards flying several feet away. Caution must be used when carbonating sweet beverages in glass and they must be stored in the fridge.

Enjoy discovering these traditional drinks, which not only create a host of beneficial bacteria for digestive ease, but taste great too.

WATER KEFIR

If you're looking for a gentle way to get used to this fermentation malarkey, then water kefir is a great place to start. It's a fantastic way to get your gut used to the new microbial visitors who are coming to take refuge. Plus you won't believe that it's good for you—the sweet taste remains from the sugar brew, but the sugar is all used up to feed the bacteria and doesn't affect you.

The origins of water kefir are a bit obscure, but they point toward either Mexico or Tibet—something to do with cacti or mysterious monks. Nothing definitive suggests where scobies came from either. Scoby is an acronym that stands for "symbiotic colony of bacteria and yeast"—in other words, a collection of yeast and bacteria that come together when the situation is right, that being sugar, moisture, and warmth, bacteria's favorite way to hang out. Making water kefir is a little like having a pet, as these scobies need food. They thrive in a specific liquid—in this case, a sugar-water-fruit liquid—and need to be fed every other day. It produces a mild, light, refreshing, slightly carbonated beverage with so many flavor options.

Those who refrain from the consumption of alcohol report a woozy, drunken feeling after drinking water kefir. While there is a very small percentage of alcohol (somewhere around 0.5 percent), an amino acid called tryptophan is created during this fermentation process. Tryptophan is eventually converted to serotonin and inspires a similar drowsy, woozy feeling, so enjoy sensibly.

The recipe below makes one quart, but if you'd like to make more or less than that, use this basic ratio: one tablespoon raw cane sugar to 1 cup filtered water and one tablespoon water kefir grains. **MAKES 1 X 1-QUART JAR**

4 tablespoons raw cane sugar (don't use honey)
....
4 cups filtered water
....
4 tablespoons water kefir grains (see page 26)

1 Dissolve the sugar in a small amount of hot filtered water, then fill the rest of a clean 1-quart jar with cool filtered water. Alternatively, you can fill the jar with hot water and let it cool to room temperature. Add the water kefir grains, then cover with a finely woven cloth or coffee filter and secure with a rubber band. Leave on the counter, ideally at 85°F, for 24 to 48 hours. Try not to leave it longer than this, as it can starve the grains (although I am guilty as charged). After 48 hours, strain the water kefir grains through a sieve and pour the liquid into another clean container, usually a bottle with a sealable lid.

2 Pop your grains back into the jar (which you have cleaned!) and feed them with some more sugary water using the ratio of one tablespoon sugar to one tablespoon water kefir grains to make a new batch of water kefir. As long as you give them sugary water on alternate days, they will flourish and you can repeat the process all over again, ad infinitum.

3 The water kefir that you have now bottled will transform into a delicious carbonated drink. You can second ferment this drink, a technical term which simply means opening up a whole playground of flavors for you to explore. Just leave $1/4$ to $1/2$ cup of room in the bottle if you want to add some flavorings.

4 To second ferment your water kefir, simply pour in some fresh fruit juice. Here are some combinations to try, but the only limits to this list are your imagination.
- Apple and cinnamon
- Coffee beans and vanilla pod
- Grape, pomegranate, and lavender
- Lemon and lime
- Mint, pineapple, lemon, and elderberry
- Rose petals and vanilla
- Tangerine and cloves

5 A word of warning, though, learned through experience: the higher the sugar content of the fruit you have added, the more carbonated (by which I mean explosive!) the drink.

6 Once you've added the juice, close the lid and leave it on the counter overnight so the probiotics in the kefir can gobble up all that new sugar.

7 Whether or not you give your water kefir a secondary ferment, you must refrigerate it. Remember, we don't want bottle bombs of your precious nectar! This will keep for up to two months in the fridge before it starts to turn tart.

COCONUT WATER KEFIR

I love every part of this fruit. If I lived in a country where coconuts were hanging on the trees, I would carry a cleaver with me at all times to hack into the delicious nectar and that fleshy white meat. Oh, how happy I would be, living in the tropics.

As perfect a drink as coconut water is, it can be given a nutritional boost by letting those hungry little water kefir grains at it. They love the stuff, as they enjoy the extra minerals it provides while reducing the sugar content for you. Sadly, most of the time I have to settle for coconut water from a carton, so putting it through a quick ferment will bring it back to life again. **MAKES 1 X 1-QUART JAR**

4 cups coconut water

4 tablespoons water kefir grains (see page 26)

1 This couldn't be easier. Pour the coconut water into a clean 1-quart jar and pop in the kefir grains. Cover with a finely woven cloth or coffee filter, secure with a rubber band, and leave to ferment for 24 hours at room temperature. The coconut water should have turned cloudy and will be probiotic-rich.

2 Strain through a sieve, collecting your grains to make a new batch. Pour the coconut water kefir into a clean bottle. You can expect it to have a sweet but tangy flavor. It's delicious with a cinnamon stick added in for extra flavor.

3 Keep refrigerated and feel free to flavor it as your imagination allows or add it to a smoothie.

COCONUT WATER KEFIR ANTI-INFLAMMATORY SMOOTHIE

If you close your eyes, you can imagine the palm trees, feel the gentle breeze, and hear the waves lapping on the beach, and know that all is well.
MAKES 1 PINT

1 medium carrot, roughly chopped

Juice from 1 lemon or orange

2 cups coconut water kefir or filtered water

2 tablespoons grated fresh turmeric (or $1/2$ to 1 teaspoon ground turmeric)

1 tablespoon grated fresh ginger

1 tablespoon raw honey or maple syrup

Pinch of freshly ground black pepper

Pinch of cayenne pepper or ground cinnamon (optional)

Place all the ingredients into a high-speed blender and whiz everything together until smooth. If your blender isn't that powerful, you may want to strain this through a fine-mesh sieve to get a smooth consistency. Drink immediately.

VIETNAMESE LEMONADE (CHANH MUOI)

I love finding a cultural reference for these fermentation techniques, so when I discovered that the Vietnamese like to make their lemonade not only sweet but salty too, I figured that a whole nation can't all be wrong and that there must be something of merit to discover, or at least try. Better still, they make it with preserved lemons (page 97), which is up there amongst my favorite ferments. Get your taste buds around this salty, sizzling tongue tickler at least once. It might even be more acceptable with a measure of gin in there!

SERVES 1

$^1/_8$ to $^1/_4$ whole preserved lemon (page 97), flesh and peel

$1^2/_3$ cups water kefir (page 280) or coconut kefir (page 282), chilled

Remove any visible seeds or spices from your lemon wedge. Place the lemon in the bottom of a glass and mash it thoroughly with a pestle or a spoon. Pour over the chilled water kefir and sip straight away. Don't forget to eat the peel at the end!

GINGER BUG

Making a ginger bug takes a little commitment, but when you see it start to bubble and become alive, it's a joy. All this effort results in a delicious, refreshing drink that is beyond satisfying and more authentic than anything you could ever find in the supermarket. **MAKES 1 X 1-QUART JAR**

GINGER BUG METHOD #1

MAKES 1 X 1-QUART JAR

3 cups filtered water

3 teaspoons raw cane sugar, plus extra for feeding

3 teaspoons diced unpeeled fresh organic ginger, plus extra for feeding

1 Combine all the ingredients in a clean 1-quart jar. Place a tight lid on the jar, give it a shake, and allow it to sit in a warm place or at room temperature. It's important that it's kept at a stable warm temperature. I tend to tuck it in near the stovetop on the counter. Plus, this way I remember to feed it too.

2 Every day for the next week, add two more teaspoons of sugar and diced ginger. The liquid will begin to get bubbly toward the end of the week. Once it's bubbly, it's ready to use. Now that it's established, the ginger bug will keep well in the fridge for a week and can be used in the lemon gingerade recipe on the next page. Give it a tablespoon of sugar every week to keep it alive.

GINGER BUG METHOD #2

MAKES 1 X 1-PINT JAR

Enough unpeeled fresh ginger to pack a 1-pint jar, roughly chopped

1 tablespoon of raw cane sugar to start, plus extra for feeding

1²/₃ cups filtered water, plus extra

1 This process is similar to making a sourdough starter and it happens over the course of five days. Loosely pack a clean pint jar with roughly chopped ginger. You can fill it to just over three quarters full. Add two tablespoons of raw cane sugar. Fill the jar to full with filtered water and pop the lid on to give it a good shake. You can leave the lid off at this initial stage to attract some wild yeasts, as you might do with your sourdough starter.

2 After 24 hours, you will need to feed this bug, so pour off a little water, feed it one tablespoon of sugar, and top it up with fresh filtered water. Put the lid on this time. Continue to do this step above for the next five days, pouring off a little water and feeding the bug every day with sugar and fresh water until it starts to bubble. Now it's ready to use in the lemon gingerade recipe on the next page.

TURMERIC BUG

You can easily incorporate more turmeric into your diet by making a turmeric bug, following the same method as the ginger bug. Make sure you buy organic, as it's a wonderfully active starter.

LEMON GINGERADE

To make delicious drinks, you can use your ginger (or turmeric) bug as the starter to get the fermentation action going in a beverage.

MAKES 1 X ½-GALLON JAR

2 lemons, peeled and sliced

4 tablespoons grated fresh ginger

6 tablespoons raw cane sugar

6 tablespoons ginger bug liquid (page 285)

Filtered water

1 Fill a clean ½-gallon jar with the lemon slices and ginger. Peeling the lemons will remove the bitter pith, which affects the taste. Add the sugar, which is purely food for the ginger bug, then add the ginger bug and fill the rest of the jar with filtered water, making sure to leave 1 inch of headspace at the top of the jar.

2 Leave to ferment for two days at room temperature, after which time you can decant into clean sealed bottles, where carbonation will build. Store in the fridge for up to one month.

LIME TURMERICADE

If you're eager to get some anti-inflammatory turmeric into you, then try this turmeric tonic. There is something about these wonder drinks that fills me with joy. I have often wished I could bottle my happiness, so perhaps this is it. Allowing the natural alchemy to take place to deliver something of such vibrant and pleasing taste really ranks up there as a sense of achievement. Or maybe it's just because turmeric is so good for you, as are the multitude of good bacteria that are created during this process. Studies reveal that these microbes can alter your mood, so go on, give it a try.

MAKES 1 X 1-QUART JAR

2 to 3 limes, peeled and roughly chopped

4 tablespoons raw cane sugar

4 tablespoons turmeric bug

Filtered water

Use the same method as outlined in the lemon gingerade recipe.

TEPACHE

I love how diving into fermentation takes you on a journey not only in your kitchen and in your body, but also around the world to taste the flavors of other cultures. Tepache tea is a Mexican drink, but I know you're thinking tequila now! It has a base of fresh pineapple, cinnamon, sugar, and water and has been drunk in Mexico since pre-colonial times. It's definitely worth a try. You need to find a ripe pineapple that's almost entirely yellow and soft to the touch and preferably organic, as you use the skin. **MAKES 1 X ½-GALLON JAR**

I very ripe pineapple (see the note above)
....
³/₄ cup raw cane sugar (panela works well)
....
3 cloves
....
I cinnamon stick
....
8 cups filtered water

1 Rinse the pineapple and cut off the top and bottom. Cut the pineapple into slices, leaving the peel on—it will help the drink to ferment and give it an interesting depth of flavor. Place the pineapple slices, sugar, cloves and cinnamon stick in a clean ½-gallon jar. Top up with the filtered water, making sure you leave 1 inch of headspace at the top of the jar.

2 Cover the jar with a tightly woven cloth secured with a rubber band and allow to ferment for two days at room temperature. If white foam has formed on top of the liquid, simply remove it with a spoon. Cover again and let it ferment for another 24 to 36 hours, but leaving it for any longer will result in vinegar—see page 322 for that!

3 Strain the tepache through a fine-mesh strainer or cheesecloth and discard the solids. If the taste is quite strong you can mix equal parts tepache with filtered water or mix it with your favorite beer à la Mexicana. Serve very cold. You can bottle it and refrigerate it for up to two months.

Whey drinks

The sweet fermented whey left behind from your adventures making labneh (see page 138) can now be made into the most refreshing, delicious, and all-round crowd-pleasing drink that you have yet to taste. This is beyond satisfying, as you waste less and create more abundance. Do note, however, that the whey used in these drinks is very different from the acidic whey left behind from traditional cheese making. Sadly, acidic whey will not make lemonade.

THE BEST BUBBLY LEMONADE

This is the most delicious lemonade I've had by far. It's also a regular feature in my kitchen, as my daughter loves to squeeze the juice from the lemons using our electric juicer. She has lots of fun and learns how to make her favorite drink.

These drinks lend themselves well to flavor combinations, so break out the rosemary and lemon or the lime and verbena. Or you can try adding some sweeter fruits beyond these citrus recipes.

- ***Orange juice*** *will give you a delightfully beneficial bubbly beverage that's similar to Orangina. You will need about three oranges per quart.*
- ***Grapefruit juice*** *is a wonderfully tangy way to start your morning.*
- ***Lime juice*** *or any mixture of citrus fruits will create a wonderful source of invaluable enzymes and bacteria to support digestion, which also just so happens to taste great.*

MAKES 1 X 1-QUART JAR

Juice of 6 lemons

$^1/_4$ cup raw cane sugar

$^1/_4$ cup sweet fermented whey (see page 140) or ginger bug (page 285)

4 cups filtered water

Pinch of ground nutmeg

1 Place the lemon juice, sugar and sweet whey in a clean 1-quart jar. Fill up with filtered water to within 1 to 2 inches of the top. It's important to leave some headspace in the jar.

2 Close the bottle and leave on your countertop at room temperature for two days to ferment. If you prefer a more tangy lemonade, you can leave the lemonade to ferment for a third day. The sugar feeds the good bacteria as it ferments and the lemonade becomes less sweet each day that you allow it to ferment. Generally three days works best for me, as I like the tang and the extra fizz.

Kvass

Traditional kvass is a drink originating in Eastern Europe. It's brewed with rye bread and dried yeasts or sourdough starter. As bread is not really a feature of my family's diet, we don't often make this type of beverage, as there are plenty of varieties using fruit and vegetables. You can make kvass from any combination of fruit, berries, and vegetables, so don't be afraid to experiment. A good example is apple, raspberry, and ginger kvass: just slice a whole apple, including the core, add a handful of fresh raspberries, and grate in about one teaspoon of fresh ginger.

HONEY KVASS

You only need fruit, unpasteurized honey, filtered water, and a few minutes to put together a delicious, homemade, health-promoting drink complete with naturally occurring vitamins, minerals, and antioxidants that will be ready in as little as two days.

Use a single fruit or a combination of fruits and feel free to experiment with herbs too. Very soft and sweet fruits (like melon, banana, mango, or papaya) ferment quicker. Need some more flavor ideas? Try these:

- *Blackberries and basil*
- *Blueberries and lemon*
- *Cranberry, apple, and lavender*
- *Dried apricots and fresh ginger*
- *Elderflower and lime*
- *Lemon balm and pear*
- *Prunes and fresh ginger*
- *Raspberry, pear, and cardamom*
- *Rhubarb, strawberry, and vanilla pod*
- *Strawberry and fresh mint*

MAKES 1 X 1-QUART JAR

Enough ripe fruit to quarter-fill a 1-quart jar

1 tablespoon raw honey

1 teaspoon other flavoring (herbs, spices, ginger, etc.—see the list above)

Filtered water

1 For raspberries or other delicate berries, put them in whole. Slice denser fruits like strawberries and apples. Halve grapes, cherries, and dried apricots, figs, or prunes. Either split or mash firm-skinned fruits like blueberries and citrus.

2 Place the fruit, honey, and optional flavoring in a clean 1-quart jar. Add enough filtered water to fill the jar almost to the top, making sure you leave 1 inch of headspace at the top of the jar. This critical head room safely allows pressure to build. There's no need to stir in the honey; it will dissolve.

3 Tightly cover the jar, set it on your countertop, and give it a gentle shake two or three times a day to prevent undesirable bacteria from forming on the surface. Allow to ferment for three days.

4 When it's ready, strain out and discard the fruit solids. Pour into a clean bottle and keep refrigerated for up to one week.

BEET KVASS

To make a simple beet kvass you just need some beets and some liquid for them to ferment in. You can either do this in a brine solution, allowing the naturally occurring probiotic strains to develop, or you can add a starter (whey or sauerkraut juice) to shorten the fermentation time. However, by adding a starter you are influencing the strain of probiotics that develop in the kvass.

You can use the beets again and make another batch of kvass by topping up the water in the jar with more 2 percent brine. When the beets start getting pale, that means they are spent and you should use fresh beets the next time. Here are a few other uses for the beets after making the initial kvass:

- *Beet tapenade (page 123)*
- *Beet kvass and sauerkraut summer soup (page 185)*
- *Beet kvass eggs (page 211)*

MAKES 1 X 1-QUART JAR

2 to 3 medium beets (golden beets are a vibrant alternative), scrubbed well

4 cups 2 percent brine solution or ¼ cup whey or sauerkraut juice + ½ tablespoon sea salt and filtered water

1 Cut the beets into cubes. Don't grate them or they will ferment too quickly, producing alcohol. Put the beets into a clean 1-quart jar—you want the jar to be about half full with beets. Add your liquid, either the 2 percent brine or filtered water plus the starter and salt. Either way, fill up the jar with the liquid, making sure you leave 1 inch of headspace at the top of the jar.

2 If you are not using a starter, let the kvass ferment at room temperature for up to three weeks. If you have used a starter, check it for taste after five days. When you are satisfied with the flavor, you can keep it in the refrigerator for up to six months. Drink diluted with water if you find the taste a little powerful at first.

PRETTY PINK SMOOTHIE

As a quick way to use kvass, I throw it into a smoothie for my kids, as anything pink clearly means yummy, in the same way that they all want the blue ice cream. ***SERVES 1***

1 cup frozen raspberries

Zest and juice of 3 oranges

1 cup beet kvass

½ cup coconut milk, nut milk, oat milk, or hemp milk

Pop everything in a blender and whiz until smooth. Top up with water until it reaches your desired consistency.

Vegetable drinks

Brewing up a healthy vegetable beverage is a great way to make a little vegetable go a long way! Favorites such as beet kvass and sauerkraut juice are commonly sold in shops throughout Eastern Europe. For some it may be love at first taste, while for others it may take a little training of the taste buds, but if chewing on a serving of sauerkraut isn't a daily desire, this is a great way to get your friendly bacteria to the party.

PROBIOTIC TOMATO JUICE

Probiotic drinks are a real treat, so why not make it as nutritious and delicious as it can be? This is a health drink of a different kind.

MAKES 1 X ¹/₂-PINT JAR

I cup whey, brine, or sauerkraut juice

I cup filtered water

I to 2 tablespoons tomato puree

Sea salt

Pinch of sauerkraut dust (page 334)

1 Blend all the ingredients together in a blender. Transfer to a clean ¹/₂-pint jar and cover with a cloth to keep any contamination out. Allow to ferment for five days, agitating it every day to stop mold from forming. It's ready when it's tangy and effervescent.

2 If you don't plan to use this drink soon, then for successful storage pour a little olive oil on top to seal the drink. This layer will solidify in the fridge and can be removed if necessary.

3 Transfer to the fridge, where it will keep for six months.

BLOODY MARY

Adjust the ingredients to suit your taste.

SERVES 1

¹/₃ cup fermented tomatoes (page 79), pureed

Juice of ¹/₂ lemon

I shot of vodka

¹/₄ teaspoon Worcestershire sauce

Ice

Celery stalk, to garnish

Lime wedges, to garnish

Pinch of kimchi dust (page 334), to garnish

Combine the tomatoes, lemon juice, vodka, and Worcestershire sauce in a jug and pour into a glass with ice. Garnish with a celery stalk, a lime wedge, and a pinch of kimchi dust.

V8 JUICE

The ultimate veggie kvass! While this savory drink might not be a priority, it makes a wonderfully complex base for a cold soup. **MAKES 1 X ½-GALLON JAR**

2 medium carrots

I celery stalk

2 small ripe tomatoes

Small handful of spinach

I spring onion

¼ small beet

2 garlic cloves

2 tablespoons fresh parsley

2 tablespoons unrefined sea salt

½ cup whey, brine, or sauerkraut juice

Filtered water

Cut all the vegetables into chunky pieces. Place all the ingredients in a clean ½-gallon jar and fill with water, making sure you leave 1 inch of headspace at the top of the jar. Put the lid on tight and ferment at room temperature for two days, then strain off the juice into fresh jars and refrigerate for two months.

Kombucha

Hello, scoby. Although you look weird, you are wonderful. The flat, rubbery disc that is at the heart of making kombucha is called a mother scoby. It essentially eats the sugar, tannic acids, and caffeine in the tea and creates a cocktail of live micro-organisms that are beneficial to us. If you're squeamish, the appearance has the potential to turn you off straightaway, but please don't deny yourself this wonderful beverage.

So what's the difference between water kefir and kombucha? Both have excellent probiotic value, but kombucha delivers a bit more goodness. Water kefir has a much faster ferment—it's ready in two days and has a sweet, mild flavor—whereas kombucha takes five to 14 days to ferment and can be a little tart. However, both can be bottled to increase carbonation and flavored whichever way you choose.

BASIC KOMBUCHA

You can easily influence the flavor of your kombucha at this initial stage because it can be made from a variety of teas. Choose from black tea, green tea, white tea, oolong tea, pu-erh tea, lapsang souchong tea, or even a mix of these. They all make especially good kombucha. Herbal teas are okay, but be sure to use at least a few bags of the above tea in the mix to make sure the scoby is getting all the nutrients it needs. Avoid any teas that contain oils, like Earl Grey or flavored teas.

Changing the sugar at the first fermentation stage will also influence the flavor. While white granulated sugar works best, you can also use pasteurized honey, palm sugar, molasses, brown sugar, and maple syrup. These will all affect the flavor as well as the brewing time: the more refined a sugar is, the quicker it will be processed and the less flavor it will add.

If you are away from home for three weeks or less, just make a fresh batch and leave it on your counter. It will likely be too vinegary to drink by the time you get back, but the scoby will be fine and you will have some kombucha vinegar to play with (see page 318). For longer breaks, store the scoby in a fresh batch of the tea base with starter tea in the fridge. Swap out the tea for a fresh batch every four to six weeks.

Kombucha will start off with a neutral aroma and then smell progressively more vinegary as it continues to brew. If it starts to smell cheesy, rotten, or otherwise unpleasant, this is a sign that something has gone wrong. If you don't see any mold on the scoby, discard the liquid and begin again with fresh tea. If you do see mold, discard both the scoby and the liquid and start fresh with new ingredients.

Finally, if you want to decrease the volume made, just apply this ratio of ingredients for a successful brew: one teabag : one tablespoon sugar : two tablespoons starter kombucha : 1 cup water. **MAKES 1 X ½-GALLON JAR**

---

¹/₃ cup raw cane sugar
....
8 cups filtered water
....
8 bags of black tea, green tea, or a mix (or 2 tablespoons loose tea) (see the note above)
....
³/₄ cup starter tea from the last batch of kombucha
....
I kombucha scoby (see page 26)

1 Add the sugar to 4 cups of boiling filtered water to dissolve it. Drop in the teabags and allow it to steep until the water has cooled. Once the tea is cool, remove the teabags (or pour the tea through a sieve to remove loose leaves) and stir in the starter tea.

2 Pour the mixture into a clean $^1/_2$-gallon jar and top up with another 4 cups of filtered water. Gently slide the scoby into the jar with clean hands. Cover the jar with a few layers of tightly woven cloth, coffee filters, or paper towels secured with a rubber band. Make sure this cover doesn't let any insects through, as they will be attracted to the sweet brew.

3 Keep the jar at room temperature, out of direct sunlight, and allow to ferment for at least seven days. It's not unusual for the scoby to float at the top, bottom, or even sideways during fermentation. However, a new cream-colored layer of scoby should start forming on the surface of the kombucha within a few days. You may also see stringy brown bits floating beneath the scoby or sediment collecting at the bottom. These are all normal signs of healthy fermentation.

4 So what happens next? After seven days, begin tasting the kombucha daily by pouring a little out of the jar and into a cup. When it reaches a balance of sweetness and tartness that's pleasant to you, the kombucha is ready to bottle.

5 Prepare and cool another pot of strong tea for your next batch of kombucha, as outlined in the first step. With clean hands, gently lift the scoby out of the kombucha and set it on a clean plate. Measure out your starter tea from your brewed batch of kombucha and set it aside for the next batch, which you can begin to make now.

6 Transfer the fermented kombucha into clean bottles using a small funnel. Keep the bottles at room temperature, out of direct sunlight, for a further one to three days if you want it to be carbonated. Refrigerate to stop the fermentation and carbonation, then drink your kombucha within a month.

JASMINE OR HIBISCUS KOMBUCHA

As it is the nature of kombucha to breed a new scoby with each brew, it's always worth claiming one to start a new brew in a different type of tea. Using the natural floral scent of a jasmine tea or a hibiscus tea is a rewarding pursuit.

MAKES 1 X ½-GALLON JAR

4 to 6 cups filtered water, plus extra to top up

4 jasmine or hibiscus teabags

2 white or green teabags

²/₃ cup raw cane sugar

I kombucha scoby (see page 26)

½ cup kombucha tea from a previous batch (page 302)

1 Pour 4 to 6 cups of boiling filtered water over the teabags in a large teapot. Allow the tea to steep for about 20 minutes, then stir in the sugar until it has dissolved. Allow the tea to cool to room temperature, then remove the teabags.

2 Pour the tea into a clean ½-gallon jar, then gently slide the scoby into the jar with clean hands. It's okay if it sinks—it will typically float up in a couple of days. Add the previous batch of kombucha tea (this helps get the culture going more quickly) and top up with room temperature filtered water, making sure you leave 1 inch of headspace at the top of the jar.

3 Cover the jar with a few layers of tightly woven cloth, coffee filters, or paper towels secured with a rubber band. Make sure this cover doesn't let any insects through, as they will be attracted to the sweet brew.

4 Allow to ferment on the countertop for seven to 17 days. After seven days, begin tasting the kombucha daily by pouring a little out of the jar and into a cup. When it reaches a balance of sweetness and tartness that's pleasant to you, the kombucha is ready to bottle. Refrigerate and drink your kombucha within one month.

LEMON GINGER KOMBUCHA

Kombucha loves a second ferment. Like the water kefir and the kvass drinks, the flavor options are endless. You can add any juice, herbs, or fresh or frozen fruit. Generally ½ cup of flavoring juice or ½ cup of fruit is sufficient. For the best results, dice or smash your fruit. The more surface area that is exposed to the liquid, the more flavor your drink will have.

Second fermentation ideas could nearly be an entirely new book, but in addition to the two recipes below for lemon ginger kombucha and spicy chai kombucha, here are some more ideas to get you started:

- *Blueberries and rosemary*
- *Chocolate and cherry*
- *Green apple, cardamom, and cinnamon*
- *Hibiscus and rose*
- *Lavender, chamomile, lemon balm, and rosemary*
- *Mango and cayenne pepper*
- *Orange, carrot, and chai spice*
- *Peach and ginger*
- *Plum and cinnamon*

MAKES 2 X 1-QUART BOTTLES

2 ounces fresh ginger (this makes enough ginger juice for 10 x 1-quart bottles)

Filtered water

Juice of 2 lemons

8 cups basic kombucha (page 302)

1 Cut the ginger into 1-inch chunks and place in a blender. Pour in enough filtered water to cover the ginger, then blend until smooth. Filter the ginger pulp by straining it through a fine-mesh strainer. This ginger juice can be frozen in ice cube trays for future batches of kombucha.

2 Prepare two clean 1-quart jars by adding three tablespoons of ginger juice and three tablespoons of lemon juice to each bottle. Top up with the kombucha, making sure you leave 1 inch of headspace at the top of the jar.

3 Seal the lids on the bottles and allow to ferment for three to five days at room temperature, then place in the fridge and drink within three months.

SPICY CHAI KOMBUCHA

This is warming, comforting, and oh so right.
MAKES 1 X 1-QUART JAR

1-inch piece of fresh ginger, cut into matchsticks

5 cloves or cardamom pods

1 cinnamon stick

1 star anise

3 cups basic kombucha (page 302)

Place the ginger, cloves or cardamom, cinnamon stick, and star anise in a large jar and cover with the brewed kombucha. Allow to second ferment for three to five days, until the flavor of the spices has infused the kombucha. If you're happy with the taste after this time, drain it through a sieve into a bottle with a sealable lid. Allow the kombucha to carbonate by leaving it out at room temperature for a week, then store in the fridge for up to three months.

CHIA KOMBUCHA

Chia seeds can be stirred into drinks, where they turn gelatinous and add a nice texture. They also deliver a boost of omega-3 fatty acids and they are wonderfully hydrating. ***MAKES 1 X 1-QUART JAR***

4 cups kombucha (page 302), any flavor

$^1/_2$ cup chia seeds

Mix the kombucha and chia seeds together, stirring well. Let it sit for one minute, then mix again. You want to allow the chia seeds to expand, but mix regularly to avoid clumping—you want a smooth texture, not lumpy. The seeds may float or sink, so stir well to disperse them evenly before serving. Chill and drink.

GREEN SMOOTHIE

Use kombucha as a base for a green smoothie.
SERVES 2

3 cups kombucha (page 302), preferably made with green or white tea

$^1/_2$ ounce kale

$^1/_4$ ounce fresh parsley

Put all the ingredients into a high-speed blender and blend until smooth.

PROBIOTIC COFFEE KOMBUCHA

Using up all this kombucha is great, but what about starting a batch of coffee kombucha? Have I got your attention now?

Note that once a scoby is used to make coffee kombucha, it will happily brew more batches of coffee kombucha for you. However, it should not be used to brew batches of kombucha tea. **MAKES 1 X ¹/₂-GALLON JAR**

8 cups freshly brewed hot coffee

¹/₃ **cup raw cane sugar**

I kombucha scoby (see page 26)

1 Pour the hot coffee into a clean ¹/₂-gallon jar and add the sugar, stirring to dissolve. Allow the coffee to cool to room temperature and make sure the coffee has no granules in it. Gently slide the scoby into the jar with clean hands. Cover the jar with a few layers of tightly woven cloth, coffee filters, or paper towels secured with a rubber band. Make sure this cover doesn't let any insects through, as they will be attracted to the sweet brew.

2 Ferment, undisturbed, at room temperature and out of direct sunlight, for at least seven days. After seven days, start tasting the kombucha daily using a straw. Stop the fermentation process when the coffee kombucha tastes pleasant by bottling your brew and storing it in the fridge for up to two months. The bottled coffee kombucha will be elevated to royal status with the addition of a vanilla pod for a second ferment.

3 Coffee kombucha should be served room temperature or cold, as heating will destroy most of the beneficial yeasts and bacteria.

Fermented honey drinks

Raw honey boasts its own little microbial profile, so using it to create a fermented drink is a natural development. There are a few refreshing drinks to explore that really come into play on a hot day, while mead has winter covered.

SWITCHEL

As you delve deeper into the world of microbes, it becomes easy to understand how active bacteria and yeast will feed off any sugar source to give you a refreshing drink. Enter switchel, a farmer's drink made with apple cider vinegar, ginger, and a variable sweetener. It's tart, fizzy, suggestively sweet, and incredibly refreshing. It even goes well with vodka—just saying!

MAKES 1 X 1-QUART JAR

4 cups filtered water

2-inch piece of fresh ginger, peeled and finely chopped

3 tablespoons raw honey, maple syrup, or blackstrap molasses

2 tablespoons raw apple cider vinegar with the mother

Zest and juice of $1/2$ lime

Place all the ingredients in a clean 1-quart jar, shake well, and place in the refrigerator overnight. To serve, pour over ice or add soda water if you'd like some extra fizz.

JUN

My children sing a song about summer that goes: "June, lovely June, thy beauty fills the ground," and oftentimes when I talk about jun (the culture, not the month), I hear this song in my head.

Jun is a fermented, refreshing tonic made of green tea and honey. I think it has a cleaner, sweeter, and less bitter taste than kombucha, with the distinct flavor of honey, making it a warm shelter of memory for me. It's expensive to make as it uses raw honey, making it a more sophisticated drink. Legend says its origins are in the Himalayas, where it's brewed by monks. My father would approve.

Here are a few other distinctive differences between jun and kombucha:

- *The jun culture **feeds on raw (unpasteurized) honey** and **green tea** rather than black tea and sugar.*
- *It **uses less concentrated tea** to brew than kombucha (half the ratio of tea to water compared to kombucha) and the tea is steeped in cooler water.*
- *Jun culture contains **a different yeast and bacteria profile**, with a higher content of Lactobacilli.*
- *It generally **brews faster** (three to six days) than kombucha, but it produces "daughter" scobies more slowly.*

All this considered, the brewing process is pretty much the same as kombucha.

MAKES 2 X 1-QUART JARS

2 bags of organic green tea or 3 tablespoons loose green tea
8 cups filtered water
¹/₂ cup raw honey
¹/₂ cup starter jun tea
1 jun scoby (see page 26)

1 Place the teabags in a clean ¹/₂-gallon jar. Boil 4 cups of the water, then let it cool to 165°F before pouring it over the teabags (brewing at higher temperatures will destroy the polyphenols in the green tea). Steep for two minutes, then remove the teabags and allow to cool further.

2 When the tea has cooled to room temperature, add the raw honey, stirring until it has dissolved. You don't add it to the warm water because you don't want to destroy the benefits of the raw honey by heating it. Add the remaining 4 cups of cold water and the starter tea (tea from your last brew).

3 Gently slide the scoby into the jar, whitest side up, with clean hands. Cover the jar with a few layers of tightly woven cloth, coffee filters, or paper towels secured with a rubber band. Make sure this cover doesn't let any insects through, as they will be attracted to the sweet brew.

4 Leave in a dark spot to ferment for between three and seven days. The amount of time needed will depend on your personal taste. The tea should be sweet with a sour tang.

5 When the jun is brewed, remove the scoby and place it in a clean bowl with the $1/2$-cup portion of jun tea reserved for brewing the next batch.

6 Pour the fermented jun tea into two clean 1-quart jars, making sure you leave 1 inch of headspace at the top of the jars. It tastes pretty perfect on its own, but jun benefits from a second fermentation using delicate flavors. If you have chosen to give it a second ferment, let the jun ferment in the bottles for another day or two more, then store in the fridge for up to three months.

7 Successful second ferments have included rose petal jun soda, lemon and lavender, or cherry and lime. Follow the directions for second fermentation as detailed in the recipe for lemon ginger kombucha on page 305.

ROSE PETAL MEAD

This is an ode to my papa, but with a further twist: he also gave me all the advice I needed to know to grow a rose! My father based his recipe on an old book written by monks, and it's a taste of childhood for me. As I write, I can nearly smell the waxy undertones of the bee. That might sound alarming, but it's an innocent story. As a young child I was the official taste tester of a mere teaspoon at any time. My honest facial expression would apparently indicate if it was ready or not.

Mead is the oldest alcoholic drink known to man. It's made from honey and water via fermentation with yeast. For many centuries mead was considered to be a veritable elixir vitae. It was widely used for digestive health and its principal medicinal value was for kidney ailments.

There is a lot more to consider when making mead than making any of the other drinks in this book. To make mead, you'll need cheesecloth, a funnel, a 2-gallon food-grade fermentation bucket, a large enough demijohn, an airlock—and patience. **MAKES APPROXIMATELY 1⅓ GALLONS**

19 cups filtered water

4 cups raw honey

8 cups fresh rose petals

1¾ cups raisins, finely chopped

Zest of 3 lemons

½ cup lemon juice

¼ teaspoon yeast nutrient

¾ ounce Champagne yeast

1 First you need to make sure that everything you are using to make your mead is sterile, including the jug and lid, the large pot, the big spoon, and the funnel. Cleaning with hot water is usually sufficient for all other ferments, but for mead, you need to make sure the water is boiling hot.

2 To begin, boil the water along with the honey for 20 minutes, skimming off any scum that accumulates on the surface. Already your kitchen will smell divine. Meanwhile, combine the rose petals, raisins, and lemon zest, and juice in your sterilized food-grade fermentation bucket. It is important that the rose petals are fresh, fragrant, and unsprayed. We don't want to be adding any undesirable chemicals to the mix. Once the honey and water have boiled for 20 minutes, pour this liquid over all the ingredients in the food-grade bucket. Stir well with a clean spoon.

3 Cover this mixture with a cheesecloth and let it cool until it reaches about 85°F. Prepare the yeast nutrient and Champagne yeast as directed by the supplier and add it to the mix. Cover again and let it sit for ten days, stirring it every day.

4 After ten days, you can strain off the mead and transfer it to a demijohn fitted with an airlock, filling it up to within 1 inch of the top. I have inherited a few of these, so it only seems right to put them to good use. This is your second stage of fermentation. Let this sit for 60 days or so. After this time, siphon it out into another sterilized demijohn fitted with an airlock. You can repeat this process a few more times, each time reducing the sediment and achieving a clear mead. Once it's clear you can bottle it into sterilized sealable bottles.

5 Lastly, add a generous portion of patience, as it takes at least a year for your honey nectar to develop in the bottle for you to enjoy.

VINEGARS

YOU DON'T HAVE to feel limited to your basic balsamic and white wine vinegars. Brew your own vinegars and delve into flavors such as zesty orange, lemongrass, and star anise vinegar or a fruity pineapple vinegar. Using the same methods outlined in this chapter, unleash your culinary creativity and get some funky infusions on the go. Some other Cultured Club favorites include blackberry and shallot; basil, lemon, and chive; summer raspberry; and pine needles and mint.

KOMBUCHA VINEGAR

A kombucha brew can taste too sweet to me, so luckily, allowing it to become vinegar couldn't be easier. Follow the instructions for making kombucha on page 302 and just let that big ol' jar of booch overbrew until all the sugar is consumed. It will take between 30 and 60 days, and then, hey presto, you've got a sweet and tasty vinegar.

Kombucha vinegar is perfect for second fermenting to create wonderful infusions that can be used for salad dressing or as a marinade. Simply add your favorite herbs and spices to your kombucha vinegar and allow it to infuse for two weeks. For example, see the recipe for the orange and rosemary vinegar on page 324.

KOMBUCHA VINAIGRETTE

Kombucha vinegar is a great base for a vinaigrette. Just strain it and combine with oil, salt, and any extra spice.

³/₄ cup extra virgin olive oil

¹/₄ cup herb-infused kombucha vinegar (see above)

I garlic clove, minced

I teaspoon ground mustard or I tablespoon fermented mustard (page II2)

Sea salt and freshly ground black pepper

Combine all the ingredients and mix well to enjoy over a salad. The dressing will keep for at least a week in the fridge.

SCRAP APPLE VINEGAR

PINEAPPLE VINEGAR

SCRAP APPLE VINEGAR

I was gifted a fun gadget that peels and cores an apple, leaving a spiralized apple. There was lots of fun, lots of apples, and all of a sudden, lots of cores and peel. Now there is lots of homemade apple vinegar. I recommend starting out with a 1-quart batch, but if you want to scale it up, use one tablespoon of raw cane sugar per 1 cup water. **MAKES 1 X 1-QUART JAR**

Peels and cores of 6 to 8 apples (you can also add pear cores, trimmings, and peels)

4 cups filtered water

4 tablespoons raw cane sugar

1 Fill a clean 1-quart jar three-quarters of the way full with apple peels and cores.

2 Pour the water into a large jug and stir in the sugar until it's mostly dissolved. Pour this over the apple scraps until they are completely covered, making sure you leave at least 2 inches of room at the top of the jar.

3 Cover loosely with a tight-weave cloth secured with a rubber band and set in a warm, dark place for around two weeks. You can give it a stir every few days if you like. If any brownish/grayish scum develops on the top, simply skim it off.

4 Once two weeks have passed, strain the scraps from the liquid. At this point, my vinegar usually has a pleasantly sweet apple cider smell, but is still missing that lovely tang. Discard the apple scraps and place the strained liquid back into a clean jar. Cover this with a tightly woven cloth secured with a rubber band and allow to ferment for another two to four weeks at room temperature until a tang develops. A little scoby, similar to your kombucha scoby, may form, which is a good thing. Congratulations! You have made your own vinegar. Transfer the liquid to a clean sealed bottle. It will keep well for six months at room temperature.

PINEAPPLE VINEGAR

Use whatever you've got for this vinegar: peels, cores, and whole fruit. Bruised or overripe fruit are fine to use too, but not anything with mold on it—that can go to the compost bin. **MAKES 1 X 1-QUART JAR**

Skin and core from 1 pineapple

2 teaspoons dried oregano

$1/4$ teaspoon chili flakes

Fruit scraps such as plums, peaches, blackberries, etc.

4 cups filtered warm water

$1/4$ cups raw cane sugar

1 Place the pineapple skin and core in a clean 1-quart jar with the oregano and chili flakes. Chop up the bigger fruit scraps, but small fruits such as berries can stay whole. Add at least a couple handfuls of fruit to the jar for a rich flavor and color.

2 Pour the warm filtered water into a large jug and stir in the sugar until it's mostly dissolved. Pour this over the fruit scraps until they are completely covered, making sure you leave at least 2 inches of room at the top of the jar.

3 Follow the method outlined for the scrap apple vinegar on page 321 for brewing the vinegar.

ORANGE AND ROSEMARY VINEGAR

Flavoring vinegars really is an opportunity to release your inner chef. This is a simple infusion that will make a great marinade or dressing.
MAKES 1 X 1-QUART JAR

I large juicy orange, chopped

4 heaped tablespoons fresh rosemary leaves

4 cups raw apple cider vinegar or kombucha vinegar (see page 318)

Place the orange pieces and rosemary in a clean bottle, then top up with the vinegar. Leave to infuse for only two to three days, then strain the vinegar into a fresh, clean bottle. Stored at room temperature, it will keep for at least six months.

ORANGE, LEMONGRASS, AND STAR ANISE VINEGAR

To give your vinegar a little more sophistication, try this wonderful combination. The Asian flavors work well as a dressing, marinade, or added at the end of a dish's cooking time to give it a burst of flavor. ***MAKES 1 X 1-QUART JAR***

4 cups raw apple cider vinegar, scrap apple vinegar (page 321), pineapple vinegar (page 322), or kombucha vinegar (page 318)

I tablespoon grated orange peel

I stalk of lemongrass

I star anise

Place all the ingredients in a clean 1-quart jar and allow the vinegar to infuse for two weeks. Strain the vinegar into smaller clean bottles and seal. It will keep for at least six months and would make a pretty nice present.

SPICE VINEGAR

This is a wonderful warm vinegar infusion that will make a great marinade. I get very excited about all the ways it could come in handy for various fermenting recipes that need a little vinegar as a starter.

MAKES 1 X 1-QUART JAR

4 cups raw apple cider vinegar or kombucha vinegar (page 318)

1 small chunk of fresh ginger, diced

2 tablespoons raw cane sugar

1 tablespoon whole allspice

1 tablespoon whole black or pink peppercorns

1 tablespoon whole cloves

1 tablespoon coriander seeds

1 teaspoon sea salt

$^1/_2$ teaspoon celery seeds

Place all the ingredients in a clean 1-quart jar and allow to infuse for two weeks, then strain into clean bottles. The vinegar will keep at room temperature for at least six months.

FOOD AS MEDICINE

FOOD HAS THE power to heal or to hurt, and the best and most efficient pharmacy is within your own body. Whole foods act as medicine to heal and protect your body, giving your immune system a break from dealing with the toxins, preservatives, additives, and chemicals that are included in so many of the foods we eat today.

It has been a long journey for me—and mostly one of rebellion!—to discover my true passion and an innate understanding of what kind of pharmacist I was meant to be. Just like my father, I have cultivated a deep desire to facilitate health, healing, and well-being, coupled with a mother's wish to provide nourishing food for my family.

I am also motivated by a deep belief in prevention over cure. By following a few simple recipes and techniques, you can brew natural probiotics in your own kitchen. And like my father, you only have to look in the garden for your cure.

While fermented foods fall under the heading of medicinal foods due to their high content of good bacteria, the additional recipes in this chapter help too. Generally they are made for medicinal purposes, so you'll need to waive any great expectations of taste! As an old Catalan proverb says, "from the bitterness of disease, men learn the sweetness of health."

MASTER TONIC

To stay healthy, we need a strong immune system to protect us. The health of your gut flora will improve your immune function, as this is where 80 percent of your immune system lives. Having a strong immune system will make your gut flora even happier, and so the loop continues. Fermented foods will help the balance of good bacteria in this delicate ecosystem, but as the many colds and flus of winter come around, it's no harm to give them a helping hand. As a winter protocol I start a batch of master tonic as a winter flu prevention that will keep the immune system strong.

After your initial brew, you can make two or three more batches from the solid ingredients. After that, you can dehydrate all the vegetable matter. Just arrange to be out of the house or at least wear goggles around your dehydrator, as that horseradish still burns! Once it's dried you can grind it into a powder and use it as a seasoning for various meals, bearing in mind that it's pretty potent. Alternatively, you can puree all the ingredients to make an interesting marinade.

The ingredients in the master tonic have been chosen for the medicinal qualities they offer.

- **Kombucha vinegar**—*probiotic, blood sugar balance*
- **Ginger**—*reduces nausea, eases digestion, and fights colds and chills*
- **Horseradish**—*antioxidant, anti-inflammatory, antibacterial, sinus clearing, coughs*
- **Onion**—*colds, bronchitis, antihistamine, high in vitamin C*
- **Garlic**—*immunity, cardiovascular health, antibacterial*
- **Jalapeño pepper**—*sinusitis, combats infection, breaks up mucus*
- **Scotch bonnet chili**—*circulation, breaks up mucus, and fever relief*
- **Turmeric**—*antioxidant, anti-inflammatory*

MAKES 2¹/₂ CUPS

I ounce fresh ginger, peeled and grated
I ounce grated fresh horseradish (be warned that this can be much stronger than onions when grating!)
I medium onion, diced
I garlic bulb, cloves diced
4 jalapeño peppers, diced
4 scotch bonnet chilies, diced
2¹/₂ cups kombucha vinegar (page 318)

OPTIONAL EXTRAS:

I lemon, sliced
I sprig of rosemary, left whole
I tablespoon ground turmeric or 2 ounces grated fresh turmeric

Place all the ingredients in a clean 1-quart jar and pour in the kombucha vinegar to cover. Leave 1 inch of headspace at the top of the jar. Close the lid and allow to infuse for at least two weeks, but steeping it for longer won't make it any stronger. Strain the liquid into a fresh clean jar—this is your master tonic. (See the note above for ideas on how to reuse the solid ingredients.) Drink a tablespoon or more each morning or when you feel the sniffles coming on.

PICKLED TURMERIC ROOT

For centuries, turmeric root has been known to have potent medicinal properties. Most notably, it's wonderful for the immune system and for reducing inflammation. Incorporate it wherever you can in your diet. You can use pickled turmeric in salad dressings or to create a super anti-inflammatory remedy. **MAKES 1 X 1-PINT JAR**

2 ounces organic turmeric root, washed, peeled, and sliced into bite-sized pieces
....
I to 3 jalapeño or red chili peppers, chopped
....
Juice of I lemon
....
2 cups raw apple cider vinegar (enough to cover)

OPTIONAL ADD-INS:
....
Thumb-sized piece of fresh ginger, peeled and sliced
....
2 to 3 whole garlic cloves
....
I cinnamon stick
....
A few whole cloves, cardamom pods, or star anise

1 Fill a clean pint jar with the fresh turmeric root and the chopped peppers of your choosing. Include any of the optional add-ins at this time too. Add the lemon juice and enough apple cider vinegar to cover the turmeric root, making sure you leave 1 inch of headspace at the top of the jar.

2 Cap the jar and place in a sunny window for one to two weeks, inverting the jar daily. Strain off the liquid into a clean jar and store in the refrigerator for up to a year.

ANTI-INFLAMMATORY REMEDY

Pour half of the vinegary mix above into a small saucepan with an equal amount of organic raw honey. Warm to incorporate the honey completely. Add one teaspoon of coarsely ground black pepper, then pour this mix back over the turmeric root in the original jar. Close the jar and allow to steep for another two weeks. Store in a cool, dark place for up to a year and eat when needed to reduce inflammation.

HONEY FERMENT FOR A COLD

This experiment is a double bonus: not only do you sweeten the lemon, but you infuse the honey with a wonderful citrus flavor. This jar is a vitamin C burst while the antibacterial honey soothes the throat. A delicious way to say goodbye to the cold. **MAKES 1 X 1-PINT JAR**

2 organic lemons, diced

1 organic orange, diced

2-inch piece of fresh ginger, peeled

1 tablespoon ground turmeric

1 cup raw honey

1 Place the lemons, orange, ginger, and turmeric in a clean pint jar with a tightly fitting lid. Pour in the honey, allowing it to settle into the gaps, then top it off again until it covers all the lemons, making sure you leave 1 inch of headspace at the top of the jar. The lemons will release a lot of juice and the mixture will be very runny. However, the lemon peel will also release pectin, a natural thickener, so it will begin to firm up. Allow to ferment for at least a month.

2 If stored in a glass jar with a tightly fitting lid in a cool place away from direct sunlight, the shelf life for this is six months. To use this medicinal powerhouse, stir a spoonful into a cup of hot water.

Kefir cleanse

If you're eager to implement ferments into your diet with a medicinal approach, try this mild yet effective cleanse over a three-week period. We all know how Elvis died, and we don't want that to be our story. This cleanse helps to remove toxins and waste from the digestive tract and the kefir helps build a balance that crowds out any undesirable bacteria.

Every morning for three weeks, make this two-ingredient blend and have it instead of breakfast.

- **Week 1**: Mix 1 tablespoon of ground flaxseed with $^1/_2$ cup of kefir.

- **Week 2**: Mix 2 tablespoons of ground flaxseed with $^1/_2$ cup of kefir.

- **Week 3**: Mix 3 tablespoons of ground flaxseed with $^3/_4$ cup of kefir.

It's very important to drink plenty of water when doing the kefir cleanse—aim for at least 8 cups a day. Excellent results are achieved with the consumption of filtered water. You can only absorb a little water at any given time, so there is no point in downing 8 cups at the end of the day. A small glass every hour is desirable, though this is a daily practice I have yet to fully master. You need this water to help your body properly flush out all the junk.

When doing this cleanse, only grind as much flaxseed as you need for that day. If you have extra, store it in the fridge to use the next morning, as freshly ground flaxseed goes rancid after a few days if left out at room temperature.

DIY probiotic powder

Fermented dust is a brilliant probiotic sprinkle for anyone who's too afraid to chew on some kimchi or fermented sprouts! Kimchi dust, sauerkraut dust, or pickle dust are all magical homemade probiotics bursting with intense flavor.

Buying a dehydrator is one of the best investments I have ever made. Some years back, I lived in a house where the kitchen was ridiculously small. It was a challenge for a family of four, as two in the kitchen was a squeeze. To further help you visualize it, the kitchen was so small that the freestanding oven/stovetop simply had to go. There was no room for the oven and all my jars.

A small slow cooker sufficed and a double-ring burner saw us through the winter. The rest of the time, the dehydrator was busy fanning away the moisture to make delicious raw treats. I had fantasized about owning one for so long, as many awkward recipes that sounded great but required five hours in the oven with the door open were now achievable and a whole new way of playing with food opened up.

I'm not saying you need to splash out on expensive equipment—one of the things I love about fermentation is how frugal it is—but once you notice your shopping bills decreasing by not buying processed products anymore, you might be able to see it as an investment, especially if you want to take your kitchen experiments—and your health—to the next level. For me, it has been more than worth it.

One thing that gives me great satisfaction is the opportunity to turn a failed project into golden dust. When left with a batch of sauerkraut that didn't taste quite right or the season's glut of zucchini pickles that had turned to mush, a stroke of inspiration landed them in the dehydrator, *et voilà*, a new seasoning was born!

Simply load up your mesh trays with your cultured foods and dehydrate them for 24 hours at 100°F. When done, transfer to a food processor and whiz to a powder. It will be intense! It will be salty, tangy, and full of goodness. A teaspoon of this powder is equal to four tablespoons of the original ferment, so you only need a little.

Use your dust as you see fit, but here are some suggestions from The Cultured Club kitchen:

- **Season** your soups, stews, stir-fries, and other dishes beginning with "s."

- Use as a **dry rub**.

- **Sprinkle** on your homemade fermented fries—it will help you get over the fact that you have cooked all the probiotics out of the potato in order to make fries!

- **Mix it** into other fermentations as a spice or starter.

- Add a pinch to that health drink known as a **Bloody Mary**!

- Add it to your **ketchup**, **mayo**, or **mustard** for extra umami.

INDEX

DEARBHLA REYNOLDS is an expert in the art of making fermented and cultured foods and is at the forefront of its current revival. It was a natural evolution for Dearbhla Reynolds to step into the role of a fermentation revivalist: she is a cross between an old-school pharmacist (her father's job) and a home economics teacher (her mother's job). She founded The Cultured Club (theculturedclub.com) as an open invitation for people to come and join in the fermenting fun, when they were ready, as opposed to being forced to eat something strange at her kitchen table. This lead to a collaboration with the Michelin star-winning OX restaurant in Belfast where she began teaching the art of fermentation. She has since developed a further range of courses with Kilruddery House and Gardens and Domini Kemp's Alchemy. Dearbhla currently lives in Holywood, Northern Ireland, with her husband and two children.